OUR HOLY FAITH

OUR HOLY FAITH

BOOK THREE

PRINCE OF PEACE

TAN Books
Gastonia, North Carolina

Originally published in 1959 as *Our Holy Faith Book III: God's Truths Help Us Live* by Bruce Publishing Company and reprinted in 1998 by The Neumann Press.

Nihil Obstat:
John A. Schulien, S.T.D.
Censor Librorum

Imprimatur:
Albert G. Meyer
Archbishop of Milwaukee
April 9, 1958

This TAN Books edition has been re-typeset and enhanced with additional content and revisions, including modernized language and updates to the practices of the Catholic Church. Catechism questions and answers have been replaced with the TAN edition of *The Third Council of Baltimore: Baltimore Catechism 1–4.*

Scripture quotes are adapted from the Douay-Rheims 1899 American Edition.

Content revisions and updates by Elisa Torres
Interior design by Caroline Green
Cover design by www.davidferrisdesign.com

ISBN: 978-1-5051-1922-0

Published in the United States by
TAN Books
PO Box 269
Gastonia, NC 28053
www.TANBooks.com

Printed in the United States of America

Contents

Publisher's Note

The original editions of the *Our Holy Faith* series textbooks were published between 1959 and 1964. They were compiled by many different authors over the course of several years. Consequently, the texts varied in their organization from year to year, with similar sections appearing with different names throughout the series and often in varying sequences.

For greater ease of use and consistency, we have reorganized each book so that the Catechism lessons, tests, and other exercises are placed at the end of each relevant chapter or lesson. We have also included answer keys for your convenience in the back of each book.

While the teachings in the original editions remain relevant due to the enduring truths of our Faith, it was necessary to update other aspects in order to more accurately reflect the Church today. These new editions have been revised to incorporate some of the changes to the practices of the Catholic Church.

To the extent possible, we have adapted the text to reflect both the ordinary and extraordinary forms of the Mass and liturgical calendars. In addition to these updates, we have inserted, where relevant to the text, traditional prayers and quotes from the Bible, the Catechism, and the saints.

This new Our Holy Faith series is faithful to the work of the original authors. It honors the fundamental and unchanging truths of the Catholic Church and is heavily influenced by tradition. We believe it is the catechesis you can trust with your children's faith.

Dear Boys and Girls

This is your religion book for this year. If you study well, you will learn many important things about your holy religion. You will learn much about God the Father, God the Son, and God the Holy Spirit. You will learn about God's love for you—how He wants you to love Him with all your heart. How He wants you to keep His commandments well, so that some day He can take you into heaven, there to be happy with Him forever and ever.

Study your lesson each day, and learn all that you can about our dear Lord. Receive Him often, if you have made your First Communion, and pray to Him every morning and evening.

Do you know any short prayers that you can whisper to our Lord and to our Blessed Mother during the day? At the end of each chapter you will find one of these. They are very beautiful and they are also very powerful prayers.

How good it is to be a Catholic! It is the Catholic Church which teaches all these wonderful things about our holy religion. Pray for others so that they too may belong to the Catholic Church. Help them find God's one true Church. Then you will not only know your religion, but you will be living it. That is what God wants you to do.

UNIT

1 I Believe In God

CHAPTER 1
We Belong to God

LESSON 1

God Made Us to Share in His Happiness

Today we see the sun, the moon, and the stars. We see the trees and the beautiful flowers. We see boys and girls. We see men and women. We see many other things. God made them all. God made everything. *God made us.*

Before the world was made there was only God. *God is the Supreme Being who made all things.*

God had nothing to start with. He made everything from nothing. How could God do this? God could make all things from nothing, because He is the Supreme Being. He is above all creatures. No one is as great as He.

Why did God make us? God made us because He is good. God made us to show forth His goodness. He wanted to show His goodness to us and to all men.

God has always been very happy in heaven. He did not need us to make Him happy, but God wanted to share His happiness. So *God made us to show forth His goodness and to share with us His everlasting happiness in heaven.* Do you share the many good things you have?

Some day, if we live as God wants us to live, we will share God's happiness in heaven. This happiness will last forever. *To gain the happiness of heaven we must know, love, and serve God in this world.*

To love and serve God means to do as He wants us to do. What does God want us to do? God wants us to be good, as He is. God wants us to obey His laws.

Before we can love and serve God, we must first know Him. How can we know God if we have never seen Him? God made it easy for us to know Him.

If we look at the world about us, everything we see will tell us that there is a God. It also tells us something about God. The sun, moon, and stars tell us how powerful He is. The trees and flowers tell us how beautiful He is. The plants which give us food tell how good God is to us. Night and day tell us how He loves us. Our own body tells us that God is wonderful and wise.

We can also know God because He spoke to some of His friends here on the earth. God spoke to Adam. He spoke to Abraham. He spoke to Moses. God spoke to many other people long before Jesus was born. In this book, we will learn about some of the people to whom God has spoken. If we look at the things God made, and learn about the wonderful things that God has told us about Himself, we will come to know and love God as our heavenly Father. When we love Him, then we will want to do the things that He wishes us to do. Then, some day, we will be happy forever in our Father's beautiful home in heaven.

Ultimately, there is no better way to know God, and to be united with Him, than to imitate and follow Jesus Christ. Hear what St. Paul wrote in the letter to the Colossians: "[Jesus] is the image of the invisible God, the firstborn of every creature: For in him were all things created in heaven and on earth, visible and invisible, whether thrones, or dominations, or principalities, or powers: all things were created by him and in him. And he is before all, and by him all things consist. And he is the head of the body, the church, who is the beginning, the firstborn from the dead; that in all things he may hold the primacy: Because in him, it hath well pleased the Father, that all fullness should dwell; And through him to reconcile all things unto himself, making peace through the blood of his cross, both as to the things that are on earth, and the things that are in heaven."

> *"The whole earth is a living icon of the face of God."*
>
> *—St. John of Damascus*

A SHORT PRAYER

O my soul, love the love that loves you from eternity.

FOR ME TO REVIEW

Catechism Lesson

1. **Q. Who made the world?**
   A. God made the world.

2. **Q. Who is God?**
   A. God is the Creator of heaven and earth, and of all things.

3. **Q. What is man?**
   A. Man is a creature composed of body and soul, and made to the image and likeness of God.

6. **Q. Why did God make you?**
   A. God made me to know Him, to love Him, and to serve Him in this world, and to be happy with Him forever in the next.

9. **Q. What must we do to save our souls?**
   A. To save our souls we must worship God by faith, hope, and charity; that is, we must believe in Him, hope in Him, and love Him with all our heart.

FOR ME TO REMEMBER

1. God is the Supreme Being who made all things.
2. God made us to show forth His goodness.
3. God made us to share His everlasting happiness in heaven.
4. To share God's happiness in heaven, we must know, love, and serve Him in this world.
5. God is our Father.

FOR ME TO DO

1. Try to love others.
2. Draw a picture showing different ways in which we can serve God.

LESSON 2

God Teaches Us How to Gain Heaven

Many years ago God the Father sent Jesus, His only Son, to become man, and to live on this earth. Jesus came to do His Father's will.

When Jesus was here, He wanted everyone to know and love His Father in heaven. That is why He taught many things about His heavenly Father to the people of the Holy Land. Jesus also taught them the things that they must do to know, love, and serve His heavenly Father.

Do you know what Jesus did so people would not forget the things that He taught? Jesus started the Catholic Church. He wanted His Church to teach the same things that He taught.

Today the Catholic Church teaches us what God wants us to know. It teaches us everything we must know and do to get to heaven. This is why we say that *we learn to know, love, and serve God from Jesus Christ, the Son of God, who is the head of the Catholic Church.*

> *"To live in heaven is 'to be with Christ.'"*
>
> *—Catechism of the Catholic Church, 1025*

Jesus taught us many things when He was here on earth. He taught these things first to His Apostles. The Apostles were the twelve men Jesus chose to help Him start the Catholic Church. They were the first priests and bishops of the Church.

The Apostles taught everything that Jesus told them. The chief things Jesus taught were put in a prayer by the Apostles. *We find the chief truths taught by Jesus Christ through the Catholic Church in the Apostles' Creed.* A creed is a short prayer which announces the most essential beliefs of Catholics and all Christians.

When we study the truths of the Apostles' Creed, we learn how great, wise, and good God is. We also learn about His wonderful love for all His children. If we know God well, we will love and serve Him in this life. We will love all His children too, near and far. Then when we die, we will live with Him forever in heaven.

A SHORT PRAYER

Sacred Heart of Jesus, I believe in Your love for me.

FOR ME TO REVIEW

Catechism Lesson

10. **Q. How shall we know the things which we are to believe?**

    A. We shall know the things which we are to believe from the Catholic Church, through which God speaks to us.

11. **Q. Where shall we find the chief truths which the Church teaches?**

    A. We shall find the chief truths which the Church teaches in the Apostles' Creed.

12. **Q. Say the Apostles' Creed.**

    A. I believe in God, the Father Almighty, Creator of heaven and earth; and in Jesus Christ, His only Son, our Lord; who was conceived by the Holy Spirit, born of the Virgin Mary, suffered under Pontius Pilate, was crucified; died, and was buried. He descended into hell; the third day He arose again from the dead; He ascended into heaven, and sits at the right hand of God, the Father Almighty; from thence He shall come to judge the living and the dead. I believe in the Holy Spirit, the Holy Catholic Church, the communion of saints, the forgiveness of sins, the resurrection of the body, and the life everlasting. Amen.

Questions

1. Who is God?
2. Why is God called the Supreme Being?
3. Why did God make us?

4. Did God make us because He needed us?
5. Will the happiness of heaven be anything like the happiness of this world?
6. Why should we always do what the Catholic Church tells us to do?
7. How can we know what we should do to know, love, and serve God?
8. Why should we want to know the Apostles' Creed perfectly?
9. Imagine that a friend, John, says that his father is on this earth just to be a good doctor. Can you prove that he is wrong?
10. Mary, a friend, can't make up her mind if there is a God or not. Can you help her?
11. How can you make God known to others?

FOR ME TO REMEMBER

1. God speaks to us today through the Catholic Church.
2. The Catholic Church teaches us to know, love, and serve God.
3. The Catholic Church teaches us God's truths.
4. The chief truths that the Catholic Church teaches are found in the Apostles' Creed.

FOR ME TO DO

1. Show your love for your classmates.
2. Find the "Apostles' Creed" in this book. Read it over to see if you are saying the words correctly. Then write it.

LESSON 3

Jesus Helps Us Know, Love, and Serve God

Jack was trying to climb a wall. He could not do it. Do you know what he did? He asked his friend to help him. With his friend's help, Jack was able to climb the wall.

> *"Courage, courage, trust in God who helps you in all things."*
>
> *—St. Mary MacKillop*

We are like Jack. We need help too. We need help to know God's truths. We need help to love and serve God. We need help to get to heaven. Who can give us the help that we need? Only Jesus, our best Friend. He will help us. He will give us help to know, love, and serve God. This help is called grace.

What is grace? Grace is a gift from God. It makes our souls holy. It helps us to do what God wants. We can enter deeper into a life of grace through prayer and the faithful reception of the sacraments.

There are two sacraments which give us much grace to know, love, and serve God. We know them already. They are the sacraments we receive when we go to confession and Holy Communion. They are called Penance and Reconciliation and Holy Eucharist. They are very important. Let us review what we know just to be sure.

A SHORT PRAYER

Christ Jesus, my helper and my Redeemer.

FOR ME TO REMEMBER

1. Jesus helps us by giving us grace.
2. God gives us grace when we pray.
3. We get grace in our souls when we receive the sacraments.
4. The sacraments of Penance and Reconciliation and Holy Eucharist give us much grace.

FOR ME TO DO

1. Write or say a prayer to Jesus. Ask Him for the grace to know, love, and serve His Father in heaven.

LESSON 4

Penance and Reconciliation—A Cure for Sick Souls

On the first Easter Sunday night, the Apostles were gathered in a big room. All at once Jesus stood before them. Do you know what He said? He said, "Peace be with you." Then Jesus breathed on His Apostles and said, "Receive the Holy Spirit. Whose sins you shall forgive, they are forgiven them." With these words Jesus gave the Apostles power to forgive sin. This is how Jesus gave us the sacrament of Penance and Reconciliation.

What is the sacrament of Penance and Reconciliation? It is the sacrament which takes away our sins. It is the sacrament we receive when we go to confession.

Why did Jesus give us the sacrament of Penance and Reconciliation? Many, many times while Jesus was on earth, sinners came to Him. Some were sorry for their sins. They asked Jesus to forgive them. Jesus forgave them their sins.

Jesus knew that after He went back to heaven, people would still sin. They would need His help to be good again. That is why He gave us the sacrament of Penance and Reconciliation.

If we commit a very bad sin (mortal sin), we know that we have rejected God's saving grace. A good confession will take away sin and reconcile us back with God. Jesus comes with His grace to live in our souls, and through confession we receive him fully back into our lives. If we confess our sins to a priest, our souls will be holy and pleasing to God again.

Venial sin is a different kind of sin than mortal sin. It does not stop saving grace from reaching our souls, but it does make us less pleasing to God. It shows we do not love God as He deserves to be loved, for God calls all of us to perfection.

Each time we receive the sacrament of Penance and Reconciliation, Jesus does something more than take away our sins. He gives us grace to be good. He helps us love Him as we should.

Jesus wants us to go to confession often. If we do, it will help us to live good, holy lives and get to heaven when we die.

> *It is called the sacrament of conversion because it makes sacramentally present Jesus' call to conversion, the first step in returning to the Father from whom one has strayed by sin.*
>
> —*Catechism of the Catholic Church*, *1423*

PRAYER

O God, be merciful to me, a sinner.

FOR ME TO REMEMBER

1. Jesus gave us the sacrament of Penance and Reconciliation on the first Easter Sunday night.
2. Penance and Reconciliation is the sacrament that takes away sin.
3. The sacrament of Penance and Reconciliation makes our souls holy and pleasing to God.
4. The sacrament of Penance and Reconciliation helps us to be good.
5. We should receive the sacrament of Penance and Reconciliation often.

FOR ME TO DO

1. All work together to write a prayer to thank Jesus for giving us the sacrament of Penance and Reconciliation.
2. Try to receive the sacrament of Penance and Reconciliation often.
3. Pray: My Jesus, have mercy!

LESSON 5

How to Receive the Sacrament of Penance and Reconciliation Worthily

Each time I receive the sacrament of Penance and Reconciliation, there are five things that I must do.

1. ***I must think of my sins.*** I must try as hard as I can to think of my sins since my last confession. The Holy Spirit will help me think of my sins. He will help me make a good confession if I ask Him for His help.

   When I think of my sins, I will find out my mortal sins first, if I have any. Then I should find out my venial sins. I do this by going over the Ten Commandments and the laws of the Church.

   I must not only think of my sins, but I must, insofar as I am capable, also know how many times I have committed each sin.
2. ***I must be sorry for my sins.*** My sins have offended God. I must make a good act of contrition to tell God that I am sorry. To have "contrition" means to be sorry for, and regret, the sins we have committed. If I am not sorry, my sins will not be forgiven. Being sorry for my sins, being contrite, is the most important part of my confession.

3. ***I must make up my mind not to sin again.*** I must genuinely intend not to sin again in the future. In relation to this, I must intend to stay away from those persons, places, or things that lead me into sin.
4. ***I must tell my sins to the priest.*** When I tell my sins I should remember that the priest is taking our Lord's place here on earth. I am really telling my sins to Jesus.
5. ***I must do or say my penance.*** The priest gives me a penance for my sins. This penance makes up for some of the punishment for my sins. I must do or say the penance the priest gives me after I leave the confessional.

   Our souls are like a bright sun after we have been to confession. They are free from sin. They are holy and pleasing to God. God dwells in them.

What to Do and Say in the Confessional

1. Kneel down and say, "Bless me, Father, for I have sinned. My last confession was (days, weeks, or months) ago."
2. Tell your sins. Tell the mortal sins first, if you have any. Then tell your venial sins. Tell the sin and the number of times you committed it.
3. When you are finished telling your sins, say, "This is all I can remember, I am sorry for these and all of my sins."
4. Father will then talk to you or ask you some questions.
5. After Father gives you your penance, say the Act of Contrition. Then leave the confessional and say your prayers. Though you may use your own words to express an Act of Contrition, the following is a formal prayer that is especially good for those learning how to say an Act of Contrition:

O my God, I am heartily sorry for having offended Thee, and I detest all my sins, because of Thy just punishments, but most of all because they offend Thee, my God, who art all-good and deserving of all my love. I firmly resolve, with the help of Thy grace, to sin no more and to avoid the near occasions of sin.

A SHORT PRAYER

Most Sacred Heart of Jesus, have mercy on us.

FOR ME TO REVIEW

Questions

1. Jordan examines his conscience every night before he goes to bed. How will this help him when he goes to confession?
2. George says that as long as he tells the priest his sins in confession, nothing else is necessary. What do you think?
3. Mark committed a mortal sin. He said that if he told God that he was sorry, he didn't have to go to confession. Is this true?

FOR ME TO REMEMBER

1. To receive the sacrament of Penance and Reconciliation worthily I must do five things:
   I must think of my sins.
   I must be sorry for my sins.
   I must make up my mind not to sin again.
   I must tell my sins to the priest.
   I must say or do my penance.
2. The most important part of going to confession is being *sorry* for my sins.

FOR ME TO DO

1. Practice writing the "Act of Contrition."
2. Resolve to go to confession regularly.
3. Say the Act of Contrition for your night prayers.

LESSON 6

The Holy Eucharist

Probably all of you have made your First Communion, and have received the Holy Eucharist.

What is the Holy Eucharist? The Holy Eucharist is the sacrament that contains the body and blood of Jesus.

At the Last Supper, the night before He died, Jesus gave the Holy Eucharist to the world. On that night Jesus said the first Mass. At this first Mass Jesus changed bread and wine into His body and blood.

He gave His priests the power to change bread and wine into His body and blood when He said to His Apostles: "Do this in remembrance of Me." At the Consecration of the Mass the priest uses this power. He changes bread and wine into the body and blood of Christ by saying the words Christ said: "This is My body" . . . "this is My blood."

Jesus loves us so much, that He stays in the tabernacle after the Mass is over. He stays there because He wants to be near us. He stays in the tabernacle because

A monstrance is used as a receptacle for which the consecrated Host is exposed for veneration.

He wants to be "our daily bread." He stays in the tabernacle so that we can come to visit Him.

Jesus wants us to come be with Him in church. When we receive Him with love, we are pleasing to God, just as the Father is "well pleased" with his Son.

> *"If angels could be jealous of men, they would be so for one reason: Holy Communion."*
>
> *—St. Maximilian Kolbe*

A SHORT PRAYER

O Sacrament most holy, O Sacrament divine!
All praise and all thanksgiving be every moment Thine.

FOR ME TO REMEMBER

1. The Holy Eucharist is the sacrament that contains the body and blood of Jesus Christ.
2. Bread and wine are changed into the body and blood of Jesus at Mass.

FOR ME TO DO

1. Make up a little prayer to say when you visit Jesus in Church.
2. At Mass, when the priest changes the bread and wine into His body and blood, say "My Lord and my God."

LESSON 7

Holy Communion—Food for Our Souls

Jesus was thinking of us, too, at the Last Supper. He knew that some day we would be living here on earth. He knew that we would need His help to be good. Jesus knew that our souls would need Him in Holy Communion. He wanted us to receive Him in Holy Communion just as the Apostles did. Did you ever see the picture of the little boy knocking at the door of the tabernacle? He wanted Jesus to come to Him. He wanted to receive Jesus.

Each time we receive Holy Communion, we receive the same living Jesus who once walked this earth. We receive the same living Jesus who is now in heaven. When we receive Holy Communion, we receive Jesus. He lives in our souls. How pure and holy our souls should be when we receive Jesus.

How much Jesus must love us to give us Himself! He comes to us in Holy Communion because He loves us. Jesus comes into our souls to give us many wonderful graces. He comes to make our souls holy. He comes to help us know, love, and serve Him better. Jesus wants us to receive Him often.

A SHORT PRAYER

Lord, I am not worthy that you should enter under my roof; but only say the word and my soul shall be healed.

FOR ME TO REMEMBER

1. Jesus wants me to receive Him as often as I can in Holy Communion.
2. I need Jesus in Holy Communion.
3. Holy Communion is the food of my soul.
4. Jesus has promised heaven to those who receive Him worthily.

FOR ME TO DO

1. Tell how your body needs food and your soul needs Holy Communion.
2. Thank Jesus for giving Himself to us to be the food of our souls.

LESSON 8

What I Must Do Each Time I Receive Jesus

Each time I get ready to receive Jesus, in Holy Communion, I must do three things:

1. *I must have my soul free from mortal sin.* If I want to receive Jesus, and I know I have committed a mortal sin, I must first go to confession. If I receive Jesus in a state of mortal sin, I commit another mortal sin.
2. *I must be fasting.* I may not eat any food, or drink anything except water, for one hour before I receive Jesus in Holy Communion. To receive Jesus when I am not fasting would be a grave sin.
3. *I must pray.* I will tell Jesus that I believe He is coming into my heart. I will tell Jesus that I love Him. I will tell Jesus that I am sorry for all my sins.

After I have said these prayers, I will keep on talking to our Lord. I will say some things to Jesus over and over again. I will say, "Jesus, I love You." "Jesus, I need You." I will try to keep thinking of Jesus. How happy I will be when Jesus comes to me! In receiving Holy Communion, I will be very devout. I will close my eyes. I will turn up my head. I will put out my tongue. When I have received Holy Communion I will bow my head for a moment until the next person has received Holy Communion.

After I have received Jesus, I will talk to Him. It is easy to talk to my best Friend. And Jesus is the best Friend of all. What should I say to Jesus? I will adore Him as my God. I will tell Him how much I love Him. I will thank Him for all the good things He has done for me. I will tell Him I am sorry for offending Him by my sins. I will ask Jesus to help me to be a better child. I will ask Jesus for the things I need. I will pray to Him for my family, for the priests, for the sisters, and for everyone.

After I have talked to Jesus for a while, I will read the prayers after Holy Communion from my prayer book, or just love Jesus quietly.

Often during the day, I will think of the happy visit that I had with Jesus. That will help me be good. Even after Jesus is no longer with me in the Blessed Sacrament, I will turn to God in my soul and praise and thank Him.

A SHORT PRAYER

The body of our Lord Jesus Christ preserve my soul unto everlasting life. Amen.

FOR ME TO REMEMBER

1. To receive Jesus worthily I must do three things:
   I must have my soul free from mortal sin.
   I must be fasting.
   I must pray.
2. I must thank Jesus when I receive Him.
3. I will try to receive Holy Communion as devoutly and as often as I can.

FOR ME TO DO

1. Prepare well for each Holy Communion.
2. Make up some prayers to say before and after Holy Communion.
3. Try to receive Jesus the next time you go to Mass.
4. Show how to go to the rail and receive Communion properly.

Write your answers on a separate sheet of paper

PART 1 Short Answer

1. Who made all things?
2. Why did God make you?
3. What must you do to share God's everlasting happiness?
4. How can you know God?
5. Why must you find out all that you can about God while you are on this earth?
6. What does it mean to serve God?
7. Who helps us to know, love, and serve God?
8. How does the Catholic Church teach us the truths about God?
9. What prayer contains the chief truths about God?
10. What is the sacrament of Penance and Reconciliation?
11. Who gave us this sacrament?
12. What five things must you do to receive the sacrament of Penance and Reconciliation worthily?
13. Which of these five things is the most important? Why?
14. Why must you tell the truth when you go to confession?
15. Why does the priest give you a penance?
16. What is the sacrament of Holy Eucharist?
17. Who gave us this sacrament? When? Why?
18. What three things must you do before you receive Holy Communion?

19. What must you do after Holy Communion?
20. What does Jesus do for your soul when you receive Him?
21. What can I do to put what I have learned to work in my daily life?

PART 2 Yes or No

Answer the following questions with Yes or No

1. Is there a Supreme Being?
2. Will the happiness of heaven ever end?
3. Does the Catholic Church teach us God's truths?
4. Am I serving God if I obey His laws?
5. Are the truths which Jesus taught the Apostles found in the Apostles' Creed?
6. Will my sins be forgiven if I am not sorry for them?
7. Is the Holy Eucharist a sacrament?
8. Must I be fasting if I wish to receive Holy Communion?
9. May I receive Holy Communion if I have a venial sin on my soul?

PART 3 Completion

Complete the following sentences by supplying the missing words

forgive	Apostles' Creed	Penance and
Catholic Church	five	Reconciliation
grace	confession	Goodness
happiness	Holy Eucharist	

1. God made me to show forth His ______ .
2. The sacrament of ______ contains the body and blood of Jesus .

3. The sacrament of ______ takes away my sins.
4. Jesus gives me ______ to help me to know, love, and serve Him.
5. The ______ contains God's truths.
6. Jesus gave His Apostles the power to ______ sins.
7. The ______ teaches me how to know, love, and serve God.
8. To make a good confession, ______ things are necessary.
9. ______ is telling my sins to the priest to have them forgiven.
10. God made me to share His ______.

Part 4 Matching

Match each term in Column I with its meaning in Column II

Column I	Column II
1. God	A. Chief truth we should know
2. Apostles' Creed	B. Not eating or drinking anything except water
3. Easter Sunday	C. Supreme Being
4. Fast before Holy Communion	D. Day on which Jesus gave us the sacrament of Penance and Reconciliation
5. Heaven	E. Reward for a good life

Part 5 Multiple Choice

Choose the correct answer.

1. Jesus gave us the sacrament of the Holy Eucharist on:
   A. Easter.
   B. Holy Thursday.
   C. Good Friday.
2. Penance and Reconciliation is a:
   A. law.
   B. commandment.
   C. sacrament.
3. The sacrament that contains Christ's body and blood is:
   A. Penance and Reconciliation.
   B. Baptism.
   C. Holy Eucharist.
4. We should receive Holy Communion to:
   A. get help to be good.
   B. make our parents happy.
   C. show people we're good.
5. God is:
   A. an angel.
   B. the Supreme Being.
   C. an apostle.

CHAPTER 2
Who and What God Is

LESSON 9

God Is a Spirit Infinitely Perfect

One day Sister said to her class, "Children, we know that God is everywhere. He is in this classroom. Why can't we see Him?"

A boy named Joe raised his hand and said, "Sister, God is a spirit. He cannot be seen with our eyes."

"That was a very good answer, Joe," said Sister. Then she continued: "Although God does not show Himself to us, we can see some of His love in the love that others show us. God loves us so perfectly that we cannot measure His great love for us. That is what we mean when we say that God is infinitely loving.

"We can see some of God's beauty about us everywhere. All the beauty that we see comes from God and shows us His beauty. That is what we mean when we say that God is infinitely beautiful. God is more beautiful than anything He has made. Nothing could be more beautiful than He is. God is infinitely perfect, too. By that we mean that God is all-perfect. We call the ways in which God is perfect His perfections. We will learn about some of His perfections in this unit."

In our last unit we learned about one of God's perfections. We learned that God is the Supreme Being. Do you know what that means? *When we say that God is the Supreme Being we mean that He is above all creatures.* He made all of them from nothing. They belong to Him.

There is no one like God. He has all perfections. He has perfections that no one else has, not even the angels. One perfection is that He is eternal. This means that God always was living and always will be living. He will never die. It also means that God will always be as great and good as He is now. So, *when we say that God is eternal we mean that He always was and always will be, and that He always remains the same.*

We have learned that God is the Supreme Being and that He always remains the same. Now let us ask: Does God know all things? Yes, God knows all things. He knows what you are doing right now. He knows what you will do after school today. He knows what you will be doing next week at this time. God knows all things, past, present, and future. There is nothing that ever happened or will happen that God does not know.

You do not know what I am thinking right now. You do not know what your mother is doing or saying at this moment. God does. He knows what all His children are thinking. He knows what they are saying and doing too. God is all-knowing. *When we say that God is all-knowing we mean that He knows all things, past, present, and future, even our most secret thoughts, words, and actions.*

God knows what is going on at every minute of the day in all parts of the world. God is everywhere. As we say in the catechism, God is all-present. *When we say that God is all-present we mean that He is everywhere.* God is not "everywhere" in the sense that everything or anything *is* God. God is everywhere in the sense that all of creation exists in and through Him at every moment;

there is nothing happening ever that God is not fully present to.

If God knows everything and is everywhere in the world, do you think He sees everything, too? Yes, God sees all things. God sees us at all times. God wants to see us at all times so He can take care of us. *God sees us and watches over us with loving care,* because He is our heavenly Father.

Did you ever watch a storm at night? What did the great streaks of lightning and the loud claps of thunder and the trees bending and breaking in the strong winds tell you? Yes, they told you of God's great power: that God can do all things; that God is greater and more powerful than anything or anyone in this world. They told you that God is almighty. *When we say that God is almighty we mean that He can do all things.* Nothing is hard or impossible for God to do. Although God is so powerful we need not fear Him if we are good.

Since God is so wonderful and great, can you see why there can be but one God?

> *Even before a word is on my tongue, Behold, O Lord, you know it altogether.*
>
> *—Psalm 139:4*

A SHORT PRAYER

My God, I love Thee.

FOR ME TO REVIEW

Catechism Lesson

13. **Q. What is God?**
    A. God is a spirit infinitely perfect.

14. **Q. Had God a beginning?**
    A. God had no beginning; He always was and He always will be.

15. **Q. Where is God?**
    A. God is everywhere.

16. **Q. If God is everywhere, why do we not see Him?**
    A. We do not see God, because He is a pure spirit and cannot be seen with bodily eyes.

17. **Q. Does God see us?**
    A. God sees us and watches over us.

18. **Q. Does God know all things?**
    A. God knows all things, even our most secret thoughts, words, and actions.

19. **Q. Can God do all things?**
    A. God can do all things, and nothing is hard or impossible to Him.

20. **Q. Is God just, holy, and merciful?**
    A. God is all just, all holy, all merciful, as He is infinitely perfect.

FOR ME TO REMEMBER

1. God is a spirit infinitely perfect.
   He is the Supreme Being.
   He is eternal.
   He is all-knowing.
   He is all-present.
   He is almighty.
2. God sees us at all times.
3. God watches over His children with loving care.

FOR ME TO DO

1. Tell God in your own words that you adore Him for all His great perfections.
2. Draw a picture of one thing that shows God's great power.
3. Learn the prayer: O God, Thou art all powerful; make me a saint.

LESSON 10

The Blessed Trinity

We all know that *there is only one God.* Now we are going to study a very deep mystery about God. A mystery is a truth we are not able to fully understand. The mystery we are going to study is a supernatural mystery. It is so wonderful that no one here on earth can fully explain it. It is such a great mystery that we could not have known about it if Jesus had not told it to us. And we cannot fully understand it even after He tells it to us. Do you know what this mystery is? It is the mystery of the Blessed Trinity.

The beginning of this mystery is seen in that God is "three in one," that God is a "Trinity." We shall never fully understand this mystery, but we must believe it because Jesus has told it to us. Have you ever seen a three-leaf clover (also known as a shamrock)? It can help us understand, if only in a small way, something about this mystery. How many leaves does a three-leaf clover have? In fact, it has three *parts* but it is only one *leaf.* This leaf reminds us of the Blessed Trinity. Do you know why? *In God there are three Divine Persons (the Father, the Son, and the Holy Spirit) but He remains only one God.*

We say that each of the three Persons is a Divine Person, because the Father, Son, and Holy Spirit are all God. Each of the three Persons of God has a special name. The first Person of the Blessed Trinity is God the Father. God the Father is called the Creator. His distinctive work is seen in the creation of the world, He is also the "Father" of creation.

The second Person of the Blessed Trinity is God the Son. God the Son, the Son of the Father, became man and is called Jesus Christ. His distinctive work is the salvation of man from sin and condemnation. Thus, Jesus is called the Redeemer.

The third Person of the Blessed Trinity is the Holy Spirit. He is also called the Sanctifier. His distinctive work is to make our souls holy with His grace.

If there are three Divine Persons in one God, is one of these Persons greater than the others? Is one more holy? No, the Son and the Holy Spirit are as great and as holy as God the Father, for they are all God. Each is one and the same God. God the Father, God the Son, and God the Holy Spirit are equal in all things. For instance, every true thing that can be said about God the Father, excepting the truth that He is the Father, can also be rightly said about God the Son.

Do you know now what we mean by the mystery of the Blessed Trinity? *By the Blessed Trinity we mean one and the same God in three Divine Persons.*

A SHORT PRAYER

Holy Trinity, one God, have mercy on us.

FOR ME TO REVIEW

Catechism Lesson

21. Q. Is there but one God?
A. Yes; there is but one God.

22. Q. Why can there be but one God?
A. There can be but one God, because God, being supreme and infinite, cannot have an equal.

23. Q. How many Persons are there in God?

A. In God there are three Divine Persons, really distinct, and equal in all things—the Father, the Son, and the Holy Spirit.

27. Q. What do you mean by the Blessed Trinity?

A. By the Blessed Trinity I mean one God in three Divine Persons.

FOR ME TO REMEMBER

1. There are three Divine Persons in one God.
2. We call the three Divine Persons in one God the Blessed Trinity.
3. The three Divine Persons in one God are equal in all things.
4. The Father is God and the first Person of the Blessed Trinity.
5. The Son is God and the second Person of the Blessed Trinity.
6. The Holy Spirit is God and the third Person of the Blessed Trinity.
7. God the Father is the Creator.
8. God the Son is the Redeemer.
9. God the Holy Spirit is the Sanctifier.

FOR ME TO DO

1. Look for signs or symbols of the Blessed Trinity in church.
2. Learn the prayer: "Act of Faith."
3. Repeat the Glory Be to the Father or make the Sign of the Cross often during the day to show that you believe in the Blessed Trinity.

LESSON 11

God Made the World

God made our wonderful world. All God did was to say, "Let there be . . ." and the things that He wanted were made. God wanted angels, and the angels were made. He wanted the earth, and it was made. God made everything from nothing. Because God made all things from nothing, we call Him the Creator of heaven and earth. *When we say that God is the Creator of heaven and earth, we mean that He made all things from nothing.*

Each thing God made is called a creature. Now let us see why God made His creatures. God made all creatures to praise and serve Him. But all the creatures He made do not share His happiness. Only the chief creatures of God were made to share in His happiness. *The chief creatures of God are angels and men.*

Angels and men praise and serve God in a way that no other creatures do. They praise their Creator with their minds, for they are able to think. They praise God with their wills, for they have free will.

A SHORT PRAYER

Teach me, O Lord, to do Thy will, for Thou art my God.

FOR ME TO REVIEW

Catechism Lesson

32. Q. Who created heaven and earth, and all things?
A. God created heaven and earth, and all things.

33. Q. How did God create heaven and earth?
A. God created heaven and earth from nothing by His word only; that is, by a single act of His all-powerful will.

34. Q. Which are the chief creatures of God?
A. The chief creatures of God are angels and men.

FOR ME TO REMEMBER

1. God is the Creator of heaven and earth.
2. God made all creatures to praise and serve Him.
3. God made angels and men to share His everlasting happiness in heaven.
4. God watches over everything He made with loving care.

FOR ME TO DO

1. Start collecting pictures of some of the things that God created. Place them in a "Creation Book" if you wish.
2. Learn the prayer: Lord, I am nothing, but although I am nothing, I adore Thee.

LESSON 12

God Made the Angels

We cannot see angels because *angels are created spirits, without bodies.* God created the angels out of nothing.

God was very good to the angels. They will never die. They have minds to know more than we can ever hope to know. They can do things no man can do. They have free will. This means that the angels are free to choose right or wrong. But best of all, God gave the angels sanctifying grace.

God wanted to give the everlasting happiness of heaven to the angels. But to get this happiness, the angels had to love and serve Him.

When God asked His angels to obey,

all the angels said they would do whatever God wanted them to do. They wanted to be faithful to Him. But *not all the angels remained faithful to God; some of them sinned and rebelled against God.*

Lucifer, the most beautiful of all the angels, said, "I will not serve." Some of the other angels that were led by Lucifer said the same thing.

Michael, the leader of the good angels was faithful to God. Many angels followed him.

There was a great battle in heaven. Because God was on the side of Michael and his angels, the faithful angels won the battle. God rewarded them. *The angels who remained faithful to God live in the eternal happiness of heaven, and these are called good angels.*

While the good angels are in heaven with God, they help us. How do they help us? *The good angels help us by praying for us, by acting as messengers from God to us, and by serving as our Guardian Angels.*

Lucifer and his angels had to be punished. *The angels who did not remain faithful to God were cast into hell, and these are called bad angels, or devils.*

Today the bad angels are still in hell. They must stay there forever. They are not God's friends any more. They have lost all the grace that God gave them. They are very unhappy. They know they will never see God again and share His happiness. They continue to rebel against God by trying to make us sin so we can be punished too.

A SHORT PRAYER

St. Michael the Archangel, defend us in battle, that we perish not in the fearful judgment.

FOR ME TO REVIEW

Catechism Lesson

35. **Q. What are angels?**
    A. Angels are pure spirits without a body, created to adore and enjoy God in heaven.

36. **Q. Were the angels created for any other purpose?**
    A. The angels were also created to assist before the throne of God and to minister unto Him; they have often been sent as messengers from God to man; and are also appointed our guardians.

37. **Q. Were the angels, as God created them, good and happy?**
    A. The angels, as God created them, were good and happy.

38. **Q. Did all the angels remain good and happy?**
    A. All the angels did not remain good and happy; many of them sinned and were cast into hell, and these are called devils or bad angels.

FOR ME TO REMEMBER

1. Angels are created spirits without bodies.
2. The angels were created to share God's happiness in heaven.
3. The good angels obeyed God; they are happy with Him in heaven.
4. The good angels help us in many ways.
5. The bad angels disobeyed God; they are unhappy forever in hell.
6. The bad angels try to make us sin.

FOR ME TO DO

1. Ask Michael, whose name means "like God," to help you fight the devil and become a better child of God.
2. Draw a picture of St. Michael driving Lucifer into hell.
3. Learn the prayer to St. Michael the Archangel.

LESSON 13

Guardian Angels

The Church believes that each created human person has a special angel called a Guardian Angel, though the Church does not teach it as an article of faith (e.g., the Trinity). Our Guardian Angels put good thoughts into our minds and strengthen our wills to do good deeds. Our Guardian Angels help us. Angels came to the aid of Jesus after his temptation in the desert. Each of us should listen to our Guardian Angel and pray to him often all our lives.

St. Therese, the Little Flower, once wrote a prayer called, "To My Guardian Angel." In this prayer she reminded her Angel of the times he came from heaven to earth to be her helper. She thanked him for his daily help. She begged her Angel to help her dear parents and all the people of the world to get to heaven. We, too, must do what St. Therese did. We must pray to our Guardian Angel for ourselves and others.

For he will give his angels charge of you to guard you in all your ways.

—Psalm 91:11

When we die, our Guardian Angel will take us back to heaven. He will say, "Here is your child, God. I have guarded him well. Please let him share eternal happiness with You in heaven."

A SHORT PRAYER

Angel of God, my guardian dear
To whom His love commits me here;
Ever this day (or night) be at my side,
To light and guard, to rule and guide.
Amen.

FOR ME TO REMEMBER

1. God gives a Guardian Angel to each of His children.
2. Our Guardian Angels pray for us.
3. Our Guardian Angels watch over us.
4. God wants us to love and obey our Guardian Angels.

FOR ME TO DO

1. Make up a little prayer to your Guardian Angel.
2. Practice writing or copying the prayer, "St. Michael the Archangel."
3. Recite the prayer to your Guardian Angel every day.

LESSON 14

Our First Parents and Their Sin

When God created the angels, He made them to share His happiness in heaven. But you remember, some of the angels lost heaven because they refused to serve God.

God also wanted to make another kind of creature. He wanted to make a creature with a body and a soul, to tend the garden in the newly created world. He wanted a creature made to His own image and likeness, to share His happiness in heaven. Who was this creature? This creature was man. What is man? *Man is a creature composed of body and soul, and made to the image and likeness of God.* The first man God made was Adam.

Because Adam was alone, God created Eve, the first woman, to be with Adam. So *the first man and woman were Adam and Eve.*

God loved Adam and Eve and gave them many wonderful gifts. Let us see what these gifts were. God gave them each a soul that would never die and filled it with sanctifying grace. A soul filled with sanctifying grace means that God is living in that soul. It was the greatest gift that God could give them. He gave them each a mind to let them learn everything He wanted them to know; a free will so they could choose to love and obey Him; a wonderful body that would never die. As long as they obeyed God, He kept pain and hunger, sickness and sadness away from them.

God wanted Adam and Eve to keep all of these gifts. He wanted us to have these same gifts, too. He wanted them to live happily in the Garden of Eden, which is also called the Garden of Paradise. But the obedience of Adam and Eve was put to the test. *God gave Adam and Eve the commandment not to eat of the fruit of a certain tree that grew in the Garden of Eden.*

Man, tempted by the devil, let his trust in his Creator die in his heart and, abusing his freedom, disobeyed God's command. This is what man's first sin consisted of. All subsequent sin would be disobedience toward God and lack of trust in his goodness.

—*Catechism of the Catholic Church*, 397

Adam and Eve did not obey the commandment of God, but ate of the forbidden fruit after they were tempted by the devil in the form of a snake. The snake provoked Eve to think in an evil way—she began to think God was not being honest with her and that God was holding back something good from her (and Adam). She disobeyed God and tempted Adam to sin too by offering him the forbidden fruit, which he then also ate of. It was a terrible sin to mistrust and disobey God, causing great unhappiness for Adam and Eve.

On account of their sin Adam and Eve lost sanctifying grace and the right to heaven, and were driven from the Garden of Eden. Heaven was closed to Adam and Eve, our first parents. It was also closed to all of us because of Adam's sin. Adam was the head of the human race. Because of "the Fall", because of our parents' first sin, the human race and all of creation became separated from perfect union with God.

God hated their sin, but He showed Adam and Eve that He did not hate them. In our next chapter, we will learn about a wonderful promise that God made to them and to us before Adam and Eve left the Garden.

A SHORT PRAYER

O Jesus, grant that I may be Thine, wholly, forever Thine.

FOR ME TO REVIEW

Catechism Lesson

39. **Q. Who were the first man and woman?**
    A. The first man and woman were Adam and Eve.

40. **Q. Were Adam and Eve innocent and holy when they came from the hand of God?**
    A. Adam and Eve were innocent and holy when they came from the hand of God.

41. **Q. Did God give any command to Adam and Eve?**
    A. To try their obedience God commanded Adam and Eve not to eat of a certain fruit which grew in the Garden of Eden.

42. **Q. Which were the chief blessings intended for Adam and Eve had they remained faithful to God?**
    A. The chief blessings intended for Adam and Eve, had they remained faithful to God, were a constant state of happiness in this life and everlasting glory in the next.

43. **Q. Did Adam and Eve remain faithful to God?**
    A. Adam and Eve did not remain faithful to God; but broke His command by eating the forbidden fruit.

44. **Q. What befell Adam and Eve on account of their sin?**
    A. Adam and Eve, on account of their sin, lost innocence and holiness, and were doomed to sickness and death.

FOR ME TO REMEMBER

1. Adam and Eve were the first man and woman.
2. God gave Adam and Eve many wonderful gifts.
3. The greatest gift that they received was sanctifying grace.
4. Adam and Eve disobeyed God.
5. God punished them for their sin.
6. God closed heaven's gates to man when Adam sinned.

FOR ME TO DO

1. Draw a picture of Adam and Eve in the Garden of Paradise.
2. Many times during the day ask God to keep your soul in sanctifying grace.
3. Act out the story of the fall of Adam and Eve.

LESSON 15

Adam's Sin Makes Us Suffer

We suffer because of Adam's sin. How? *On account of the sin of Adam we come into the world without sanctifying grace, and we inherit "original sin."* Let us see what this means.

When we came into this world we had Adam's sin within our souls, as well as its bad effects (especially death). *We did not personally commit this sin ourselves, but because we are united spiritually with the parents of the human race, we inherit the condition of sinfulness when we are conceived.* If Adam had not sinned we would not have to die. But now all men must die. This sin, if not taken away by God, prevents us from being with God in heaven when we die. Original sin makes it hard for our minds to know right from wrong and to understand many things. This sin also makes it hard for us to be good. Even our bodies suffer because of this sin of Adam. Sometimes they get sick. They get tired. We have pains and aches.

Adam's sin causes us suffering. But God has offered the perfect help for our sinful condition. He has given us Baptism. When we are baptized, original sin is removed from our souls. Once original sin is gone, and if we do sin mortally after baptism, sanctifying grace is in our souls to help us know and do what is right. God comes to live in our souls. He makes us His children and enables our souls to live with Him in heaven. God is good. If we sin again, sanctifying grace is restored to our souls by confession, by the sacrament of Penance and Reconciliation.

If Adam had not sinned, our bodies would never have suffered or died. All of natural creation was damaged by the sin of Adam. Because of this, many times during our lives we have to suffer even if our own original sin is taken away. But suffering can bring us closer to God, and we have a helper in Christ, who Himself is called "the suffering servant." If we suffer willingly for the sake of righteousness, we prepare our souls for heaven and become more like Christ. Our bodies will die, it is true, but on the last day they will rise from the dead. They will be united with our souls to live with God forever if we believe in and follow our Savior, Jesus Christ. There is one human person that was free from original sin. *The Blessed Virgin Mary was free from original sin.* God gave Mary this special favor, because He knew that some day

she would be the mother of the Redeemer. *This favor is called her Immaculate Conception.* This means that from the very start of Mary's life, her soul was filled with grace. Mary's Immaculate Conception made her the most perfect and holy vessel for giving birth to, and caring for, Jesus.

Original sin is not the only kind of sin; there is another kind, called "actual sin," which we ourselves commit.

In the next part we will learn about actual sin.

A SHORT PRAYER

O Mary, conceived without sin, pray for us who have recourse to thee.

FOR ME TO REVIEW

Catechism Lesson

45. **Q. What evil befell us on account of the disobedience of our first parents?**

    A. On account of the disobedience of our first parents, we all share in their sin and punishment, as we should have shared in their happiness if they had remained faithful.

46. **Q. What other effects followed from the sin of our first parents?**

    A. Our nature was corrupted by the sin of our first parents, which darkened our understanding, weakened our will, and left in us a strong inclination to evil.

47. **Q. What is the sin called which we inherit from our first parents?**

    A. The sin which we inherit from our first parents is called original sin.

48. **Q. Why is this sin called original?**
A. This sin is called original because it comes down to us from our first parents, and we are brought into the world with its guilt on our soul.

49. **Q. Does this corruption of our nature remain in us after original sin is forgiven?**
A. This corruption of our nature and other punishments remain in us after original sin is forgiven.

50. **Q. Was any one ever preserved from original sin?**
A. The Blessed Virgin Mary, through the merits of her Divine Son, was preserved free from the guilt of original sin, and this privilege is called her Immaculate Conception.

FOR ME TO REMEMBER

1. We suffer because of Adam's sin.
   a) We are born with original sin on our souls.
   b) We are born without sanctifying grace.
   c) It is hard for us to know right from wrong.
   d) It is hard for us to understand many things.
   e) It is hard for us to be good.
   f) Our bodies must suffer and die.
2. The Blessed Virgin Mary was free from original sin.
3. We did not commit original sin; we commit actual sin.

FOR ME TO DO

1. Say this little prayer to Mary:

"By thy Immaculate Conception, O Mary, make my body pure and my soul holy."

LESSON 16

Actual Sin

There is a story in the Bible which shows that the children of Adam and Eve inherited original sin. It is the story of Cain and Abel.

Cain and Abel were sons of Adam and Eve. Cain was a farmer and Abel was a shepherd. Abel was good and loved God very much. But Cain became wicked. .

One day Abel built an altar to make a sacrifice. He put his very best lamb on the altar and offered it to God. Because Abel was good God was pleased with his gift.

Cain offered a gift to God, too. He burned some fruit on an altar. Because Cain did not do his best for God, God was not pleased with his gift.

Cain became angry and envious of Abel. He hated his brother so much that he killed him. God punished Cain for his sin. He had to leave home and spend his days wandering around the earth.

Cain's sin was an actual sin. What is actual sin? *Actual sin is any willful thought, desire, word, action, or omission forbidden by the law of God.* Let us see what these big words mean.

If I willingly think of something that God's law tells me is wrong to think about, then I commit an actual sin. Willingly thinking unkind or impure thoughts would be sinful. If a girl had an accident and I said to myself "It serves her right" I am unkind to her in my thoughts.

If I willingly desire or wish something sinful, then that would be an actual sin. If I wish that I could steal my friend's baseball, that is a sinful desire.

If I willingly speak in a way that God's law forbids, then those words are sinful. It is sinful to use God's holy name the wrong way.

If I willingly do something that God prohibits, then I commit an actual sin. Stealing is a sinful action.

If I willingly omit doing something that God's law tells me I must do, then that is a sin. God, through His Church, tells me to go to Mass on Sunday. If I omit going to Mass on Sunday because I am lazy, then I commit an actual sin.

Actual sin, then, is anything that I think, wish, say, do, or omit that God forbids.

How many kinds of actual sin are there? *There are two kinds of actual sin: mortal sin and venial sin.*

A SHORT PRAYER

From all sin, deliver me, O Lord.

FOR ME TO REVIEW

Catechism Lesson

52. **Q. What is actual sin?**
    A. Actual sin is any willful thought, word, deed, or omission contrary to the law of God.

53. **Q. How many kinds of actual sin are there?**
    A. There are two kinds of actual sin—mortal and venial.

FOR ME TO REMEMBER

1. Actual sin is anything I willingly think, wish, say, do, or omit that is against God's law.
2. There are two kinds of actual sin: mortal and venial sin.

FOR ME TO DO

1. Draw a picture of the sacrifices made by Cain and Abel.
2. Write a three-sentence story about Cain and Abel.
3. Offer little acts of love to God today.

LESSON 17

Mortal Sin

What is mortal sin? *Mortal sin is a serious offense against the law of God that cuts our soul off from sanctifying grace.* Remember, we can sin against God's law by thinking, wishing, saying, or doing something God does not want us to do, or by omitting something He commands us to do. If the thought, desire, word, action, or omission is a very great offense against God's law, and if we know this, and if we do it with the full consent of our will, it is a mortal sin.

The word "mortal" means deadly. If we eat a deadly food, we die. If we commit a mortal sin, the life of grace in our soul dies. This does not mean that the soul dies, because our souls will never die. Our souls will live forever. So when we say *this sin is called mortal because it takes away the life of the soul,* we mean it takes away the life of grace in the soul.

If we lose sanctifying grace by committing a mortal sin, are we still God's friends? No, a soul in mortal sin is an enemy of God, because to commit mortal sin is to rebel against God. Therefore, mortal sin is the worst evil in the world.

Sometimes boys and girls do not understand about mortal sin. Not all sins are mortal sins. *To make a sin mortal, these three things are necessary:*

First, *the thought, desire, word, action, or omission must be seriously wrong or considered seriously wrong. The Church calls any action that is seriously wrong a "grave matter."* This means that the sin must be a "big" sin. It must be very wrong. If you shoot and kill a person on purpose, it is a grave sin. If you miss Mass on Sunday through your own fault, that is a grave sin.

Second, *the sinner must know it is seriously wrong.* This means that you must know it is a grave sin before you do it. If a very small child takes something off the store shelf and mindlessly puts it in his pocket before leaving the store, does he commit a mortal sin? No, you must know that the sin is a grave sin when you are doing it, and the child in this case was not aware he was stealing.

Third, *the sinner must fully consent to it.* This means that you must want to commit the sin and do it willingly. Missing Mass on Sunday is a grave sin. You know it is a grave sin to miss Mass on Sunday. But you miss Mass because even though you are fully awake, you are too lazy to get up. Did you commit a mortal sin? Yes, because you willingly stayed away from Sunday Mass.

It is important to understand that only when *all three* of these things are true about a person's action does a person commit a mortal sin. For instance, if a bad action is ***not*** a grave matter, but one does it knowingly and with full consent, this is not a mortal sin.

Mortal sin destroys the life of grace in the soul. It displeases God. It offends Him very much. But if you are sorry for the mortal sin and confess your sins to God through the sacrament of Penance and Reconciliation, God can take that mortal sin off your soul and become your friend once more.

If I ever commit a mortal sin, what should I do? I should say an act of contrition at once and tell the sin in my next confession.

> *"Where sin was hatched, let tears now wash the nest."*
>
> *—St. Robert Southwell*

A SHORT PRAYER

Jesus, deliver me from mortal sin.

FOR ME TO REVIEW

Catechism Lesson

54. Q. What is mortal sin?
A. Mortal sin is a grievous offense against the law of God.

55. Q. Why is this sin called mortal?
A. This sin is called mortal because it deprives us of spiritual life, which is sanctifying grace, and brings everlasting death and damnation on the soul.

56. Q. How many things are necessary to make a sin mortal?
A. To make a sin mortal three things are necessary: a grievous matter, knowledge that it is a grievous matter, and full consent of the will.

FOR ME TO REMEMBER

1. Mortal sin is a great offense against the law of God.
2. Mortal sin can keep me out of heaven forever.
3. Mortal sin takes away the life of grace from my soul.
4. I must hate mortal sin more than anything else in the world.
5. Three things are necessary to make a sin mortal:
   It must be a grave sin.
   I must know it is a grave sin before I do it.
   I must willingly do it.
6. Mortal sin can be forgiven if I am sorry for it.

FOR ME TO DO

1. Write a prayer to Jesus, asking Him to keep you free from mortal sin.
2. Say the "Act of Contrition" every night to tell Jesus you are sorry for all of your sins.
3. Write the "Act of Contrition."
4. Learn the little prayers: From all sin, deliver me. O Lord, be merciful to me, a sinner.

LESSON 18

Venial Sin

Billy and Bobby were very good friends. They played together every day. But Bobby made fun of Billy. This hurt Billy and when it happened over and over, Billy and Bobby were no longer good friends.

Venial sin keeps us from being a close friend of God. It keeps us from getting all the graces that God wants us to have. If we keep committing venial sins over and over again, without telling God that we are sorry and that we still love Him, we will find we are less willing to do what He wants us to do. We will love Him less and less.

What is a venial sin? *Venial sin is a less serious offense against the law of God.* This means that venial sin, like mortal sin, is an offense against the law of God. True, venial sin is not as great an offense against God's law as a mortal sin is. It does not drive God from our souls. But it offends God who loves us so much.

When is a sin a venial sin? *A sin can be venial in two ways:* first, *when the evil done is not seriously wrong; second, when the evil done is seriously wrong, but the sinner sincerely believes it is only slightly wrong, or does not give full consent to it.* Now, let us see what this means.

Quarreling with your little brother is not seriously wrong. This is a venial sin. If you became quite angry and injured his body seriously in the fight, this could be a mortal sin, but if you sincerely believed it was only slightly wrong when you did it, the sin would be venial. Suppose your anger led you into a fight and you hurt your brother seriously before you realized what you were doing; then you committed a venial sin because you did not give your full consent to that grievous sin.

Now do you know the difference between mortal sin and venial sin? Go over it again to be sure.

Does venial sin take away sanctifying grace? No, venial sin does not take away sanctifying grace, but it offends God; it makes us less pleasing to Him and brings a punishment with it. That is why we must try to keep away from venial sin.

Is it necessary to go to confession to have venial sins forgiven? No, it is not necessary to go to confession to have our venial sins forgiven, but it is well to do so.

Venial sin can also be forgiven by assisting at Mass devoutly; by receiving Holy Communion; by praying; by making little sacrifices and by doing acts of kindness for others.

A SHORT PRAYER

My Jesus, mercy!

FOR ME TO REVIEW

Catechism Lesson

57. Q. What is venial sin?

A. Venial sin is a slight offense against the law of God in matters of less importance, or in matters of great importance it is an offense committed without knowledge of its seriousness or full consent of the will.

58. Q. Which are the effects of venial sin?

A. The effects of venial sin are the lessening of the love of God in our heart, the making us less worthy of His help, and the weakening of the power to resist mortal sin.

FOR ME TO REMEMBER

1. Venial sin offends God.
2. Venial sin makes us less pleasing to God
3. We must try to stay away from all sin.

FOR ME TO DO

1. Go to confession soon to become a close friend of Jesus.
2. Say the little prayer, "My Jesus, mercy!" often during the day.
3. Make a list of little sacrifices that you can do to please Jesus.

LESSON 19

How to Practice Virtue

If we ask God for His help when we assist at Mass and when we receive the sacraments, God will give us grace to fight temptations.

One way for us to avoid sin and temptations is by staying away from the persons, places, or things that may cause us to sin. Persons, places, or things that may lead us into sin are called *near occasions of sin.* God tells us to stay away from all occasions of sin.

If we commit the same sin over and over again, we say we have a bad habit. How can we break a bad habit? We can break a bad habit by doing the opposite good thing. If we tell lies over and over again, we have the bad habit of lying. We can avoid lying and practice a good habit by telling the truth. God will give us grace to turn all of our bad habits into good habits if we ask Him for His help. If we keep doing good things over and over again, our bad habits will soon disappear. These good habits done for the love of God are called virtues and should be practiced for the love of God. God loves us when we practice little virtues.

God hates sin. That is why He has given us so many helps to avoid sin. But God is just. If we do not make use of the helps He gives us to avoid sin, He will punish us. If we do use them, and remain good, He will reward us.

A SHORT PRAYER

Jesus, my God, I love Thee above all things.

FOR ME TO REVIEW

Questions

1. Name three ways in which God shows us that He watches over us with loving care.
2. Name three prayers in which the Blessed Trinity is mentioned.
3. Ned thinks that God the Father is the greatest Person of the Blessed Trinity. Do you agree?
4. Fred wants to explain to a friend what Catholics mean by the Blessed Trinity. What can he tell his friend?
5. Imagine someone that has a habit of stealing a penny now and then. He justifies himself by saying that stealing a penny is just a venial sin. What would you tell him?
6. Which of these things will keep you from committing sin?
   a) Praying for God's grace every day.
   b) Spending free time with others who sin or encourage sin.
   c) Disobeying your teacher.
   d) Receiving Holy Communion often.
   e) Being kind to other children.
   f) Watching shows or movies that celebrate sinful behavior.
   g) Disobeying your parents.
   h) Telling lies.
7. If you have committed a mortal sin and desire forgiveness, what should you do? How? Why?
8. How can bad habits be replaced by good habits?

FOR ME TO REMEMBER

1. God's grace will always keep me from committing sin if I receive it while living faithfully and obediently.
2. I form good habits by practicing virtue.
3. God will reward me if I am good.
4. God will punish me if I am bad.
5. God is a just God.

FOR ME TO DO

1. List some good habits you would like to have.
2. List some bad habits you want to replace with good habits.
3. Say the Our Father with special attention to the part "and lead us not into temptation."
4. Learn some short prayers for time of temptation.

Write your answers on a separate sheet of paper

Part 1 Short Answer

1. How perfect is God?
2. What does infinitely perfect mean?
3. Name some perfections of God.
4. What word do we use to show that God has no beginning and will never die?
5. Why didn't God have a beginning?
6. How much does God know?
7. Where is God?
8. Why does God want to be looking at His children all day long?
9. What does almighty mean?
10. How does God show us that He is almighty?
11. Is there only one God?
12. How many Persons are there in God?
13. What is the Blessed Trinity?
14. Who is the second Person of the Blessed Trinity?
15. Who is the first Person?
16. Who is the third Person?
17. Which Person is called the Sanctifier?
18. Which Person is called the Creator?
19. Which Person is called the Redeemer?
20. Why is God called the Creator?
21. Why are we called creatures?
22. Who are the chief creatures of God?
23. Why are they called God's chief creatures?
24. Did God make the angels before He made the earth?
25. Did God make the angels to be greater than men?
26. What kind of work do the good angels do?
27. What do the bad angels do?
28. Name some gifts that Adam and Eve received from God.

29. What was the most important gift that Adam and Eve received?
30. How did God test Adam and Eve?
31. How did God punish them?
32. What do we call Adam's sin in us?
33. How do we suffer from Adam's sin?
34. How do we get Adam's sin off our souls?
35. Who is the only human person that was free from original sin?
36. What is this favor called?
37. What is actual sin?
38. How many kinds of actual sins are there?
39. What is mortal sin?
40. Why must we avoid mortal sin?
41. What is venial sin?
42. Who will help us keep from sin? How?
43. If God is patient with us and all the sins we commit against Him, will He expect us to be patient and to forgive others?
44. How can we apply what we have learned to our own lives?

Part 2 Matching

Write 1 to 10 on another paper. After each number write the letter which is in front of the correct answer.

1. God the Son	A. Sanctifier
2. Blessed Trinity	B. can't be seen with our eyes
3. God the Father	C. Redeemer
4. Spirit	D. Three Persons in one God
5. God the Holy Spirit	E. Creator
6. Immaculate Conception	F. a beautiful garden
7. Original sin	G. first man
8. Devil	H. Adam's sin in us
9. Paradise	I. bad angel
10. Adam	J. Mary was free from Adam's sin

Part 3 Completion

Write 1 to 20 on another paper. Find the correct word for each sentence from the list.

sees	God	mortal sin
second	The Blessed Virgin	angels
secret	Mary	original
Divine	venial	soul
spirit	things	prayers
Father	actual	happiness
Redeemer	sanctifying grace	mystery

1. The chief creatures of God are men and ______ .
2. Angels and men were created to share God's ______ .
3. The good angels help us by their ______.
4. Your ______ makes your body live.
5. The greatest gift that Adam received was ______.
6. The sin we inherit from Adam is called ______ sin.
7. Sins we commit are called ______.
8. ______ takes away all the grace from our souls.
9. ______ was free from original sin.
10. _____ sin is a lesser offense against God's law.
11. God can do all ______.
12. God the Son is the ______ Person of the Blessed Trinity.
13. God is a ______ infinitely perfect .
14. God ______ me all the time.
15. God takes care of us because He is our heavenly ______.
16. There are three ______ Persons in God.

17. Only ______ can make things from nothing.
18. God the Son is called the ______.
19. The Blessed Trinity is a ______.
20. God knows even my most ______ thoughts.

Part 4 Yes or No

Answer each question with yes or no.

1. Is God the Holy Spirit as holy as God the Father?
2. When we say that God is all-present, do we mean that God will live forever?
3. Did God the Son redeem us?
4. Can we hide anything from God?
5. Will God live forever?
6. Are angels spirits?
7. Did the angels have to earn their place in heaven?
8. Was the Blessed Virgin free from all sin?
9. Must we try to stay away from all sin?
10. Does venial sin take away our grace?
11. Will we be punished for our sins?
12. Does mortal sin make us lose our right to heaven?
13. Is a venial sin a grave sin?
14. Do we have to earn our place in heaven with God's grace?
15. Did we have sanctifying grace in our souls when we were born?

UNIT 2 I Believe in Jesus Christ

CHAPTER 3

God the Son Becomes Man to Save Us

LESSON 20

God Promises a Savior to Adam

You remember that, after they sinned, Adam and Eve became broken and lost their original harmony with God and themselves. They no longer could remain in paradise, and without grace, heaven was closed off to them. Everything might have looked dark and hopeless for Adam now, but God is always quick to forgive and come to our aid.

God did not abandon man after Adam fell into sin, and ultimately God did something wonderful. He *promised to send into the world a Savior to free man from his sins and to reopen to him the gates of heaven.*

The Savior would be Jesus. The name Jesus means Savior. He would save all men from hell. By dying on the cross, He would redeem them. He would throw open the gates of heaven which had been closed. In this way, He would be both our Savior and our Redeemer.

> *I will put enmity between you and the woman, and between your seed and her seed; he shall bruise your head, and you shall bruise his heel.*
>
> *—Genesis 3:15*

Did God send the Savior to the world as soon as Adam sinned? No, God was going to make men wait thousands of years before the Savior would come. The righteous people of the Old Testament looked forward to Jesus' coming, and like John the Baptist, prepared His way.

What happened, then, to the people who died before the Savior came? If they were good and were sorry for their sins, God forgave them. He put into their souls some of the grace that Jesus would earn later on when He died on the cross.

In this way they could be saved, but they could not go to heaven until Jesus took them there because the gates of heaven were closed. Where did the souls of these people go to wait for Jesus? These souls went to limbo, a place of waiting; when Jesus died on the cross, He descended into limbo to save the souls who awaited their salvation.

A SHORT PRAYER

O Jesus, be to me a Savior.

FOR ME TO REVIEW

Catechism Lesson

60. **Q. Did God abandon man after he fell into sin?**
    A. God did not abandon man after he fell into sin, but promised him a Redeemer, who was to satisfy for man's sin and reopen to him the gates of heaven.

61. **Q. Who is the Redeemer?**
    A. Our Blessed Lord and Savior Jesus Christ is the Redeemer of mankind.

FOR ME TO REMEMBER

1. God promised Adam that He would send a Savior to the world.
2. Men had to wait thousands of years for the coming of the Savior.
3. Jesus is our Savior and Redeemer.

FOR ME TO DO

1. Write a prayer to thank God for promising a Savior to the world.
2. Draw a picture that shows God promising the Savior to Adam.
3. Write a three sentence story about your picture.

LESSON 21

God Makes His Promise to Others

Adam and Eve remembered God's promise. This promise filled them with hope. They tried to be good. Some of their children were good. Others forgot God's promise and became very wicked. God looked upon the good people and was pleased with them. These He called His children. God made the Jews His Chosen People.

God told some of the great leaders of His Chosen People about this promise of a Redeemer. He also told them many things about the Redeemer who was to come.

Abraham was the father of God's Chosen People. He was a very holy man. He loved God very much. Abraham's faithful obedience was proven, so God made him the father of all His people. God showed him the land in which he wanted His Chosen People to live. This land was called the Promised Land.

Abraham was the father of God's Chosen People.

God told Abraham that He would bless him with many children. From these children would come the Savior of the world.

Many years passed by, and Abraham died. Later God's Chosen People suffered very much in the land of Egypt. They were being used as slaves. So God chose another great leader for them. This leader was Moses. Moses was told to take the Hebrews out of slavery in Egypt and into the Promised Land. God gave Moses the commandments to tell the people how they should live.

God also told King David that the Savior was coming. God said that the Savior would come from David's family. David was very happy to hear this news. He wrote many beautiful songs about the coming of the Savior. We call these songs the Psalms, which are recorded in the Old Testament.

A SHORT PRAYER

Jesus, Son of David, have mercy on me.

FOR ME TO REMEMBER

1. Abraham was the Father of the Chosen People.
2. Moses kept the hope of a Redeemer alive in the hearts of his people.
3. God promised King David that the Savior would come from his family.

FOR ME TO DO

1. Find and read the stories of Abraham, Moses, and King David in the Bible.

LESSON 22

Man Prepares for the Redeemer

For thousands of years, people waited for the Savior to come. We will learn how they prepared for Him.

God wanted the Jews to prepare for the Savior by believing that He would come to redeem them. That is why He told so many people that the Savior was coming.

The Jews also prepared for the Savior's coming by prayer. Each day the people asked God to have mercy on them. They begged God to hurry and send the Savior. During Advent we are supposed to do the same thing.

Since the Jews were God's special friends, He commanded that they prepare for the Savior by obedience. Each time the Hebrews obeyed God they were rewarded. But when they disobeyed, God punished them.

Another special way in which God's people prepared for the Savior's coming was by offering sacrifice. In the time before Christ, sacrifice is offering God a gift, or a victim, such as a lamb. This victim was offered to God by a priest. The priest made the offering for all the people who shared in the sacrifice. The victim was placed on an altar. If it was an animal it was killed, and its blood was sprinkled on the altar. The victim was then burned. The burning showed that the sacrifice was to be offered to God alone, and the sacrifice had four special reasons:

to adore Him,
to thank Him,
to make up for sin, and
to ask God for His favors.

Sacrifice in the Old Testament prepared humanity for the final and perfect sacrifice, that of Jesus Christ on the cross. Christ is the sacrificial "lamb" that redeems the whole world.

A SHORT PRAYER

Lamb of God, who takes away the sins of the world, grant us peace.

FOR ME TO REMEMBER

1. Man prepared for the coming of the Savior by faith, prayer, obedience, and sacrifice.
2. To offer a sacrifice to God three things are necessary: a priest, a victim, and an altar.
3. A sacrifice is offered for four reasons: to adore God, to thank Him, to make up for sin, and to ask God for His favors.

FOR ME TO DO

1. Draw a picture showing the High Priest offering a lamb in sacrifice to God.
2. Make a list of the things that you wish to do to prepare for the coming of the Savior on Christmas.

LESSON 23

God Keeps His Promise—The Annunciation

"Dear God, send us a Savior!" This was the prayer that was said for many years before the Savior was to come.

Some people not only prayed for the Savior to come, but also wished that He would be born in their family.

Mary, the holiest and best of all women, also prayed that the Savior would soon come to the world. But she never asked God to let the Savior be born into her family. She thought that she was not worthy of such a great favor.

One day Mary was alone. Suddenly she looked up. The Angel Gabriel was standing before her.

The Angel began to speak. "Hail, full of grace," he said. "The Lord is with thee. Blessed art thou among women." Do you see now that the beginning of the Hail Mary prayer was taught to us by an angel? Mary was frightened. Why had the angel come? Why was he saying these words to her?

The Angel Gabriel spoke again. "Don't be afraid, Mary. You have found favor with God. You shall have a Son. You shall call His name Jesus. He shall be great and shall be called the Son of the Most High."

Mary listened to the angel. She knew that God had sent him to her. The angel told her that God wanted her to be the Mother of the Redeemer. Mary bowed her head and said, "Behold the handmaid of the Lord. Be it done to me according to thy word."

Because the angel had said, "He shall be called the Son of the Most High," Mary knew that her Son was the Son of God.

God knew that Mary and Jesus, His Son, should have someone to look after them. St. Joseph, a very holy and good man, took Mary for his wife. He was happy to have such a holy and good wife.

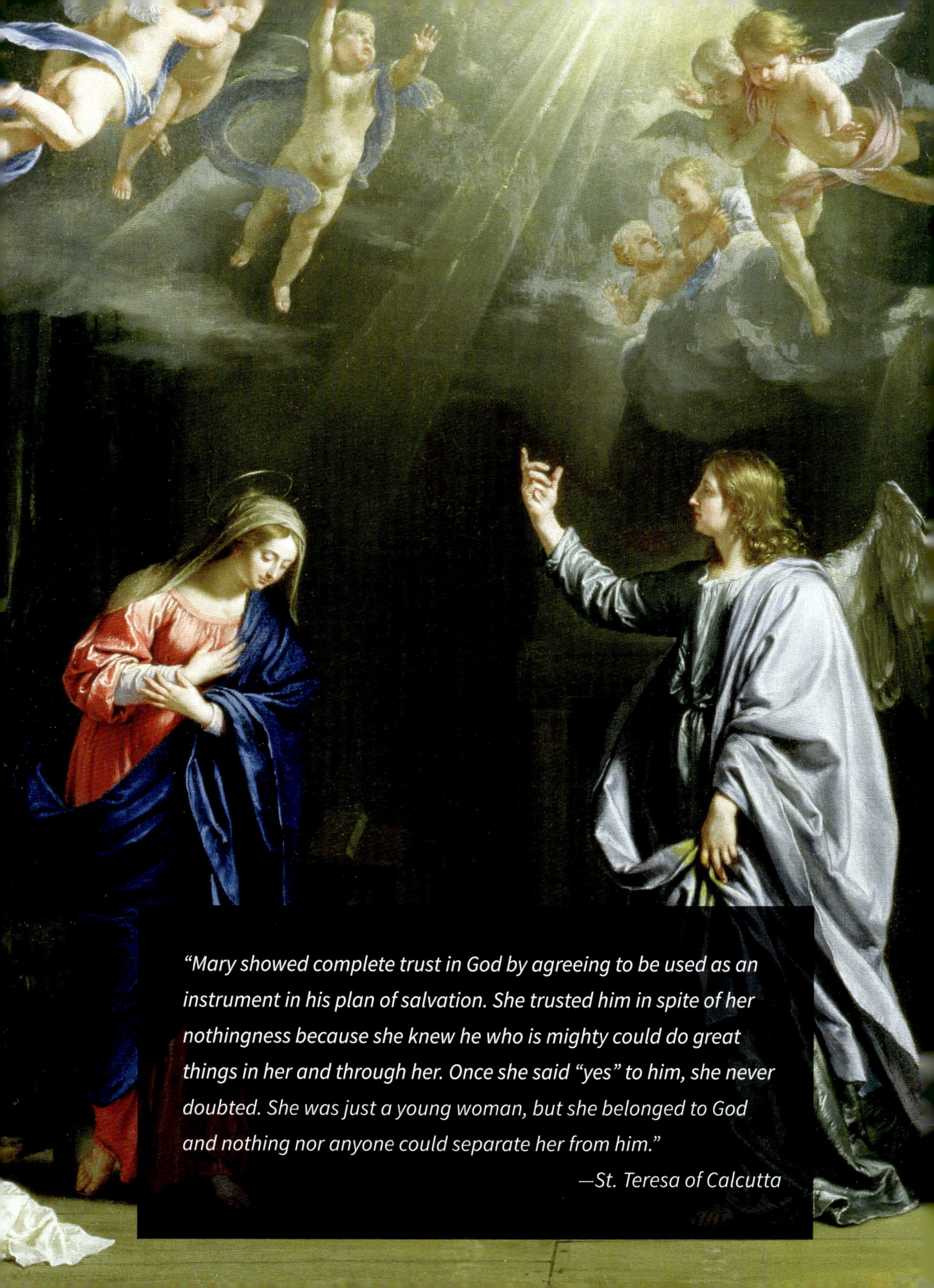

"Mary showed complete trust in God by agreeing to be used as an instrument in his plan of salvation. She trusted him in spite of her nothingness because she knew he who is mighty could do great things in her and through her. Once she said "yes" to him, she never doubted. She was just a young woman, but she belonged to God and nothing nor anyone could separate her from him."

—St. Teresa of Calcutta

A SHORT PRAYER

My Mother, my Hope.

FOR ME TO REMEMBER

1. God sent the Angel Gabriel to Mary.
2. God sent the Angel Gabriel to ask Mary to be the Mother of the Savior.
3. St. Joseph was the husband of Mary and the foster father of Jesus.

FOR ME TO DO

1. Learn and say the prayer, "The Angelus."
2. The Angel Gabriel honored Mary when he spoke the first words of the Hail Mary. Honor Mary often by saying the same prayer to her.

LESSON 24

Mary Visits Elizabeth

Before the Angel Gabriel left Mary, he told her that her cousin Elizabeth was going to have a son. Mary was happy when she heard this news. She knew that for many years Elizabeth had begged God to send her a son.

Elizabeth lived far away from Mary's home. It would take Mary about four days to make the trip, but Mary decided to visit her. She knew that God would be pleased if she helped her cousin Elizabeth.

Elizabeth saw Mary coming and at that very moment the Holy Spirit let her know that Mary was to be the Mother of the Savior. Elizabeth greeted her cousin with these words, "Blessed art thou among women, and blessed is the fruit of thy womb. Who am I that the mother of my Lord should come to me?" Mary answered her cousin with a beautiful song (which the Church calls the Magnificat) in which she praised God. Mary was happy that God had chosen her to be the Mother of His Son.

After her visit with Elizabeth, Mary went back to her home in Nazareth.

A SHORT PRAYER

Blessed are thou, O Virgin Mary, by the Lord God most high, above all women upon the earth.

FOR ME TO REMEMBER

1. Elizabeth was Mary's cousin.
2. The Holy Spirit let Elizabeth know Mary was to be the Mother of the Savior.

FOR ME TO DO

1. Make up a song to praise God for His goodness to you.
2. Draw a picture for your room showing Mary's visit to her cousin Elizabeth.
3. Listen carefully to the beautiful song Mary sang to Elizabeth.
4. Imitate Mary by being very humble.

LESSON 25

The Birth of Our Savior

Mary and Joseph were not in their own little home when Jesus was born. Do you know the reason why?

The Roman governor was making a list of all the people who lived in his country. Mary and Joseph had to make a long and tiresome trip to Bethlehem to put their names on the governor's list. Many other people had to go to Bethlehem to do the same. Every house in Bethlehem was filled with these travelers. So were the inns.

Joseph knew that he had to find a place for Mary, because she was very tired from her long journey. He also knew that it was soon time for the Savior to be born.

At last Joseph found a cave on a hillside. Mary and Joseph spent the night there. During the night, when the cave was dark and still, God's own Son came to earth.

Mary took Jesus "and wrapped him in swaddling clothes, and laid him in the manger, because there was no room for them in the inn." How happy Mary and Joseph were for they were the first to adore the newborn Savior. Heaven and earth rejoiced when *Christ was born of the Blessed Virgin Mary on Christmas Day, in Bethlehem, more than two thousand years ago.*

A SHORT PRAYER

My God and my all.

FOR ME TO REVIEW

Catechism Lesson

75. Q. On what day was Christ born?

A. Christ was born on Christmas day in a stable at Bethlehem, over two thousand years ago.

FOR ME TO REMEMBER

1. Jesus was born in Bethlehem more than nineteen hundred years ago.
2. Jesus was born in a cave, because no one had room for Him.

FOR ME TO DO

1. Tell the story of the birth of Jesus to your parents.
2. Try to be as obedient to your parents as Mary and Joseph were to the rulers of their land.
3. Write a prayer to Jesus, telling Him that you will make room for Him in your heart on Christmas Day.

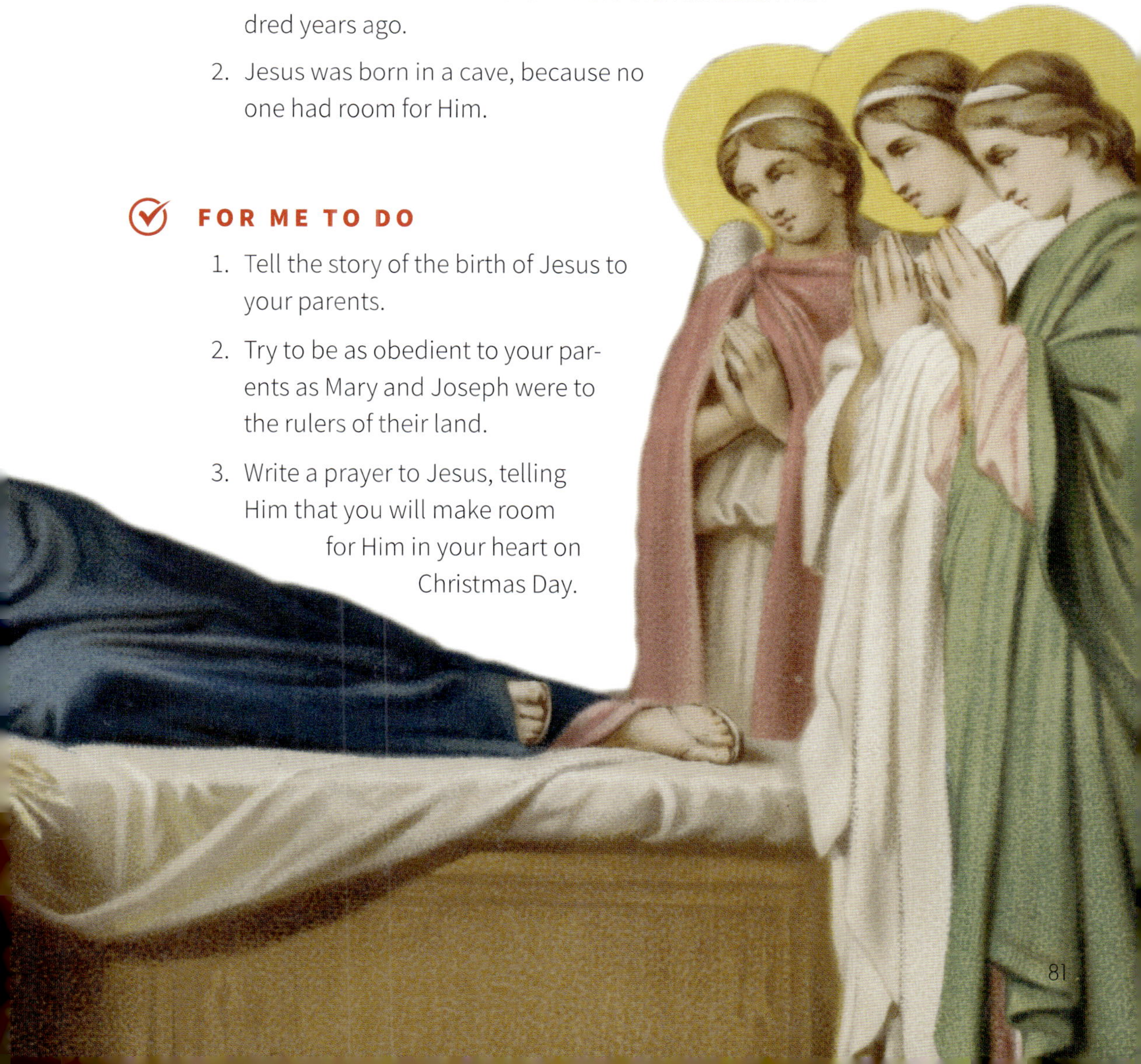

LESSON 26

The Shepherds at the Crib

Did all of the people of Bethlehem go to the cave to see the Savior as soon as He had come? No, the people did not know that the Savior was near them. God did not send His angel to tell them the good news. He sent an angel to some poor shepherds who were watching sheep on a hillside.

The angel said to them, "Do not be afraid, for behold, I bring you good news of great joy which shall be to all the people; for today in the town of David a Savior has been born to you who is Christ the Lord. And this shall be a sign to you: you will find an Infant wrapped in swaddling clothes and lying in a manger."

As soon as the angel had given the message, many other angels appeared in the sky. They sang, "Glory to God in the highest, and on earth peace among men of good will."

When the angels left, the shepherds said to one another, "Let us go over to Bethlehem and see this thing that has come to pass, which the Lord has made known to us."

There they found Mary and Joseph, and the babe lying in the manger just as the angel had told them. They knelt down and adored Jesus. Then they went away glorifying and praising God. They told all the people whom they met about the birth of the Savior.

A SHORT PRAYER

Blessed be Jesus Christ and His most pure Mother.

FOR ME TO REMEMBER

1. An angel told the shepherds that Jesus was born.
2. The shepherds went to visit Jesus.
3. They told others what they had seen.

FOR ME TO DO

1. Write a report about what you think the shepherds might have done when they visited Jesus.
2. Draw a picture that tells the story of the angel's visit to the shepherds.
3. Make or cut out a crib for your bedroom.

> *Teacher of children became himself a child among children, that he might instruct the unwise. The Bread of heaven came down to earth to feed the hungry.*
>
> *—St. Cyril of Jerusalem*

LESSON 27

Jesus Is Presented in the Temple

When Jesus was forty days old, Mary and Joseph took Him to the great Temple in Jerusalem. This was what the law required. As faithful people, Mary and Joseph went to show us how to be obedient. At the Temple they offered Jesus to God. They also made an offering of two turtle doves, the gift of the poor.

While Mary and Joseph were in the Temple, they met a holy old man named Simeon. Simeon had prayed for years, asking God to let him live to see the Savior. When Simeon saw Jesus, he knew at once that He was the Savior. He took Jesus in his arms and held Him lovingly. Then he sang a beautiful song of praise to God. Now all priests say this prayer to God every day.

Simeon also had some sad news for Mary that day. He told her that she would have great sorrow in her life. Mary never forgot the words of Simeon.

A SHORT PRAYER

Virgin most sorrowful, pray for us

FOR ME TO REMEMBER

1. Jesus was offered to God when He was forty days old.
2. A holy old man named Simeon told Mary that she would have great sorrow in her life.

FOR ME TO DO

1. Write or tell a story of Mary presenting Jesus to God in the Temple.
2. When you go to Mass offer yourself to God.
3. Learn about the Seven Sorrows of the Blessed Virgin Mary.

LESSON 28

The Wise Men Worship the Savior

After Jesus was born Wise Men came from the East to adore Him. These Wise Men were also called Magi. They liked to study the stars. When Jesus was born they saw a new star in the sky. This star was brighter than all the other stars. When they saw the star they knew that the time had come for Jesus, the Savior, to be born.

The Wise Men started on a long journey across the desert on camels to find the Savior. The bright star moved in the sky and showed them the way.

When the Wise Men reached Jerusalem, the star disappeared. So they went to King Herod and asked about the new King. King Herod had not heard about Him.

Herod told them to go to Bethlehem and find Him. Then they should come back and tell him where He was.

As soon as the Magi left Herod's palace, they saw the star again. It guided them to the house where Jesus was. "And entering the house, they found the Child with Mary His Mother and falling down they worshipped Him. And opening their treasures they offered Him gifts of gold, frankincense, and myrrh. And being warned in a dream not to return to Herod, they went back to their own country another way."

A SHORT PRAYER

Bless us, Mary, Maiden mild,
Bless us, too, her tender Child

FOR ME TO REMEMBER

1. The Wise Men knew that Jesus was born, because they saw His star in the sky.
2. The Wise Men visited Baby Jesus.
3. They gave Him gifts of gold, frankincense, and myrrh.

FOR ME TO DO

1. Would you like to be a little Wise Man? Then each time that you receive Jesus in Holy Communion offer Him these gifts:
   a) The gold of love,
   b) The frankincense of your prayers,
   c) The myrrh of your little penances.

LESSON 29

Life at Nazareth

One night when St. Joseph was sleeping an angel appeared to him. He told Joseph to take Jesus and Mary to Egypt at once. He also told Joseph about King Herod's plan to kill Baby Jesus because Herod was afraid that the people would make Jesus their king when He grew up. St. Joseph obeyed the angel. The Holy Family lived in Egypt until Herod died. Then an angel told Joseph to return to his own country.

The Holy Family left Egypt. They went to live in Nazareth. The house was a very simple one, like the other houses there. Here the Holy Family prayed, and worked, and played together.

St. Joseph worked hard every day in a little carpenter shop. Jesus often helped him in many ways. Can you think of some things that Jesus did for His foster father?

Mary took care of the house. Jesus often helped His mother with her work. Jesus was always kind, helpful, and obedient at home. He wanted to show us how we, too, must act at home if our family is to be happy. How can your family be as happy as that of the Holy Family?

A SHORT PRAYER

Jesus, Mary, Joseph.

FOR ME TO REMEMBER

1. The Holy Family went to Egypt to escape King Herod.
2. When the Holy Family left Egypt, they went to Nazareth to live.

3. The Holy Family had a very happy life in Nazareth.
4. By His good example Jesus showed us how to obey.

FOR ME TO DO

1. Draw a picture of Jesus helping St. Joseph in the carpenter shop. Add this picture to your wall display.
2. Talk about the Holy Family at prayer.
3. Find a picture of Nazareth or research the Holy House of Loreto.

LESSON 30

The Child Jesus in the Temple

On great feast days, Mary and Joseph went to the Temple in Jerusalem to offer sacrifice to God.

When Jesus was twelve years old, He was allowed to go to Jerusalem with His mother and foster father to celebrate a great feast. The feast lasted for seven days. During this time, thousands of animals were sacrificed to God.

When the feast was over Mary and Joseph joined a large number of their friends and relatives and started back to Nazareth. Jesus stayed in Jerusalem.

When evening came, Mary and Joseph discovered that Jesus was not with the group. Where was He? Mary and Joseph turned back and looked for Him.

On the third day they went to the Temple. There they found Jesus "sitting in the midst of teachers, listening to them and asking them questions." These men did not understand how a twelve-year-old boy could know so much, especially since He was only a carpenter's son.

Mary asked Jesus why He stayed in the Temple. He answered, "Did you not know that I must be about My Father's business?" Then Jesus left the Temple and went back to Nazareth with Mary and Joseph and obeyed them. He stayed there until He was thirty years old.

The finding of Jesus in the temple is the only event that breaks the silence of the Gospels about the hidden years of Jesus. Here Jesus lets us catch a glimpse of the mystery of his total consecration to a mission that flows from his divine sonship: "Did you not know that I must be about my Father's work?" Mary and Joseph did not understand these words, but they accepted them in faith. Mary "kept all these things in her heart" during the years Jesus remained hidden in the silence of an ordinary life.

—*Catechism of the Catholic Church*, 534

A SHORT PRAYER

O Jesus, the friend of little children, bless the children of the whole world.

FOR ME TO REMEMBER

1. Mary and Joseph found Jesus in the Temple when He was twelve years old.
2. Jesus returned to Nazareth and obeyed Mary and Joseph.
3. Jesus lived at Nazareth until He was about thirty years old.

FOR ME TO DO

1. Draw a picture of Jesus with the teachers in the Temple.
2. Describe the caravan going back to Galilee after the Passover.
3. Talk about being obedient.

LESSON 31

Jesus Is God Made Man

The Savior of all men is Jesus Christ. Jesus Christ is God. But He is man too. *The chief teaching of the Catholic Church about Jesus Christ is that He is God made man.*

If Jesus is both God and man, is He two persons? *No, Jesus Christ is only one Person; and that Person is the second Person of the Blessed Trinity.*

Each one of us is one person. We have one nature, called a human nature. It is our human nature to have a body and a soul. We can act and think as a human being, because it is the nature of a human being to act and think. We can laugh and cry. We can suffer.

Jesus also had a human nature. He had a body and soul like ours. That means that when He was here on earth He could think and act as we do. He sometimes got hungry. He could suffer, too. In many ways, Jesus showed that He had the nature of a man, a human nature.

We have only one nature, a human nature. Jesus has two natures, a human nature and a divine nature. Jesus has a divine nature, which means that He is God, almighty, all-knowing, and eternal. He has a human nature, which means He is a human being. But He is only one person, God the Son, the second Person of the Blessed Trinity. He became man when He came on earth. But He is a divine Person.

We see then that Jesus has two natures, divine and human. That means that He can act as God and as man. But He is still only one Person. All His actions are the actions of a Divine Person.

If someone asks you how many natures Jesus Christ has, what would you say? You would say that the Church teaches that *Jesus Christ has two natures: the nature of God and the nature of man.*

In our next unit, we will learn more about the life of Jesus. We will see that Jesus showed His two natures. He showed that He is God by working miracles. He showed that He is man by doing the same things that we do, by eating, working, sleeping, and growing up.

A SHORT PRAYER

Thou art the Christ, the Son of the living God.

FOR ME TO REVIEW

Catechism Lesson

62. **Q. What do you believe of Jesus Christ?**
    A. I believe that Jesus Christ is the Son of God, the second Person of the Blessed Trinity, true God and true man.

65. **Q. How many natures are there in Jesus Christ?**
A. In Jesus Christ there are two natures, the nature of God and the nature of man.

66. **Q. Is Jesus Christ more than one person?**
A. No, Jesus Christ is but one Divine Person.

Questions

Tell which of these things you can do to thank Jesus for coming to save us from hell:

1. Say your morning and night prayers daily.
2. Keep everything you get just for yourself.
3. Help those who are in trouble.
4. Play fair in all your games.
5. Tell the truth at all times.
6. Obey your parents willingly and at once.
7. Be attentive at the Mass.
8. Pray for those whom you do not know.

FOR ME TO REMEMBER

1. Jesus Christ is God.
2. Jesus is Man.
3. Jesus is God made man.
4. Jesus is only one Person.
5. Jesus has two natures: the nature of God, and the nature of man.

FOR ME TO DO

1. Make a large rosary on the bulletin board with colored circles. For the large beads, try to find pictures to illustrate the five Joyful Mysteries.
2. Make a visit to the Blessed Sacrament to thank Jesus for letting us know that He is both God and man.

Write your answers on a separate sheet of paper

Part 1 Short Answer

1. To whom did God make the first promise of a Redeemer?
2. Name two other people who were promised that the Savior would come.
3. Did men have to wait a long time for the Savior?
4. How did men have to prepare their hearts for the Savior?
5. What is a sacrifice?
6. What is necessary to offer a sacrifice?
7. For what reasons can a sacrifice be offered?
8. How did Mary find out that she was to be the Mother of the Redeemer?
9. Who was Elizabeth?
10. Where was Jesus born?
11. How long ago was Jesus born?
12. Who were the first ones to visit Jesus?
13. What gifts did the three Wise Men give to the Savior?
14. How old was Jesus when He was offered to God in the Temple?
15. Where was the Temple?
16. What holy man told Mary that she would have great sorrows in her life?
17. Why did the Holy Family go to Egypt?
18. What was the name of the King who tried to kill Baby Jesus?

19. Who told Joseph that King Herod was dead?
20. Where did Jesus live until He was about thirty years old?
21. What can we learn for our own lives from the life of the Holy Family at Nazareth? From Jesus? from Mary? from Joseph?

Part 2 Yes or No

Answer each question with yes or no.

1. Did people have to wait a long time for the Savior to come?
2. Did an angel tell the three Wise Men that Jesus was born?
3. Did King Herod try to kill Baby Jesus?
4. Was Jesus born at Nazareth?
5. Does Jesus have two natures?

Part 3 Completion

Write 1 to 5 on another paper. Find the correct word for each sentence from the list.

altar
priest
Elizabeth
Mary
Gabriel
Adam
Angel
Eve

1. The shepherds were told of Jesus' birth by an ______.
2. To offer a sacrifice, we need a victim, an ______, and a priest.
3. The Angel ______ asked Mary if she would be the Mother of Jesus.
4. ______ was the first to whom the Redeemer was promised.
5. ______ was the name of Mary's cousin.

Part 4 Multiple Choice

Answer 1 to 4 on your own paper as you did before with the letter A or B or C.

1. Jesus was taken to the Temple and offered to God when He was:
   A. forty years old.
   B. forty days old.
   C. six years old.
2. The prayer that reminds us of the Annunciation is:
   A. the "Our Father."
   B. the "Angelus."
   C. the "Apostles' Creed."
3. The Wise Men found Jesus because they followed:
   A. a star.
   B. an angel.
   C. a cloud.
4. As a boy, Jesus lived in:
   A. Jerusalem.
   B. Bethlehem.
   C. Nazareth.

Part 5 Matching

Write 1 to 10 on another paper. After each number write the letter which is in front of the correct answer.

1. Herod	A. The Mother of the Redeemer
2. Elizabeth	B. Tried to kill Baby Jesus
3. King David	C. The Savior of the world
4. Mary	D. Mary's cousin
5. Gabriel	E. Wrote songs about the coming of Jesus
6. Jesus	F. Was the land of the Jews
7. Simeon	G. Asked Mary to be the Mother of God
8. Abraham	H. The birthday of Jesus
9. Christmas	I. Prayed to see the Savior
10. Promised Land	J. Offered sacrifice to God

CHAPTER 4
Jesus Dies for Us

LESSON 32

Jesus Begins His Public Life and Work

When Jesus was about thirty years old, He left His home at Nazareth to do the work His Father sent Him to do. What was this work? He was to teach the people about His Father in heaven. He was to teach the people how to live. But most of all He was to redeem the world by suffering and dying on the cross. In this way, He could make up to God for the sins of all men.

Before He began His work, Jesus went to the River Jordan to see His cousin, John the Baptist. John was preaching penance to the people and baptizing them. He wanted to help them get ready for the Redeemer when He came.

Jesus listened to the words that His cousin was saying. When the time came for the people to be baptized, Jesus stood in line with the others.

At last it was Jesus' turn to be baptized. John looked at Him. He knew that this was Jesus, the Savior of the world. How did John know this? The Holy Spirit helped him to know.

At first John did not want to baptize Jesus but when Jesus asked him to do it he immediately obeyed.

Then something wonderful happened. The Bible tells us: "The heavens were opened to him, and he saw the Spirit of God descending as a dove and coming upon him. And behold, a voice

from the heavens said, ‘This is my beloved Son, in whom I am well pleased.’”

Here in the River Jordan, our Holy Redeemer was shown to us as the Son of God, in the beautiful mystery of the Blessed Trinity. God the Father speaks from heaven. God the Holy Spirit comes in the form of a dove. God the Son is baptized and hears His Father say: “This is my beloved son.”

A SHORT PRAYER

Thy will be done.

FOR ME TO REMEMBER

1. St. John the Baptist was Jesus' cousin.
2. John "baptized" Jesus in the River Jordan.
3. God the Father and God the Holy Spirit were present at the "baptism" of Jesus, who is God the Son.
4. The presence of the three divine Persons at the baptism of Jesus reveals the Blessed Trinity.

FOR ME TO DO

1. Consider how you can thank God for making you His child at baptism.
2. Learn the words that the priest used when you were baptized. "I baptize you in the name of the Father, and of the Son, and of the Holy Spirit."
3. Draw a picture of the baptism of Jesus in the River Jordan.
4. Find and read this story in the Bible.
5. Make a list of the things you can do every day to make yourself pleasing to God.

LESSON 33

Jesus Is Tempted by the Devil

After Jesus was baptized, He went into the desert to pray and fast before He began His work.

At the end of forty days, Jesus was very hungry. The devil came to tempt Him.

Because Jesus was hungry, the devil said to Him, "If you are the Son of God, command that this stone become a loaf of bread."

Jesus did not obey the devil, so the devil tried to tempt Him again.

This time the devil took Jesus to the top of the temple. He said to Jesus that if He were the Son of God, He should throw Himself down because angels would keep Him from falling to the ground.

Jesus said, "You shall not tempt the Lord your God."

Then the devil showed Jesus all the kingdoms of the world. He said, "All of this shall be yours if you fall down and adore me."

Jesus said to Satan, "Go away from here. The Lord your God should you adore. Him only should you serve."

If Jesus was tempted by the devil, we must expect to be tempted by him too.

A SHORT PRAYER

Deliver me, O Lord, from mine enemies.

FOR ME TO REMEMBER

1. Jesus prayed and fasted for forty days in the desert.
2. The devil tempted Jesus.
3. We must treat the devil as Jesus did.

FOR ME TO DO

1. Draw a picture of Jesus being tempted by the devil.
2. Act out the story of Jesus in the desert.
3. Ask Jesus to send the devil away whenever he tries to make you sin.

LESSON 34

Jesus Chooses His Apostles

Another day, Jesus passed by the River Jordan. John the Baptist was talking to two of his followers, Andrew and John. When he saw Jesus, John the Baptist said, "Behold the Lamb of God." At once Andrew and John left John the Baptist and went with Jesus. These two fishermen were the first followers of Jesus.

Then Andrew took his brother Simon to Jesus. Jesus said, "Your name shall not be Simon, but Peter." Do you know why Jesus changed Simon's name to Peter? Peter means "rock," and Jesus had plans for Peter in which he would need to be as strong as a rock. Now Peter was a follower of Jesus too.

The next day Jesus started on His return to Galilee, and saw Philip. Jesus invited Philip to follow Him too.

In this way Jesus went about choosing His twelve Apostles. Some day He may call you, as He did the Apostles. Will you do as the Apostles did? You must pray for the grace to do God's will.

> *God did not tell us to follow Him because He needed our help, but because He knew that loving Him would make us whole.*
>
> *—St. Irenaeus of Lyons*

A SHORT PRAYER

Queen of the Apostles, pray for us.

FOR ME TO REMEMBER

1. Jesus chose twelve men to be His helpers and special friends.
2. These men were called the Apostles.
3. The names of the twelve Apostles are: Peter, Andrew, James, John, Philip, Jude, Bartholomew, Matthew, Thomas, Simon, James the Less, and Judas.

FOR ME TO DO

1. Read the story of Jesus calling the twelve Apostles.
2. Can you memorize the names of the twelve Apostles?
3. Tell how we can be helpers of Jesus, like the Apostles.

LESSON 35

The Wedding Feast at Cana

One day, Jesus and His Mother were invited to a wedding feast in the little town of Cana.

Many guests came to the feast. Soon all the wine was gone.

The servant in care of the wine was excited and worried. What would happen if the guests found out that there was no more wine?

Mary saw what was happening, and she whispered to Jesus, "Son, they have no wine."

Jesus told the servants to fill six large stone pots with water. The servants filled them to the brim. Then Jesus said, "Draw out now, and take to the chief steward." The servants obeyed.

The chief servant tasted it. The water had been changed into wine. It was better wine than he had served before. He did not know where it came from. He called the bridegroom and said, "Every man at first sets forth the good wine, and when they have drunk freely, then that which is poorer. But you have kept the good wine until now."

This was the first miracle that Jesus worked. He worked this miracle to please His mother.

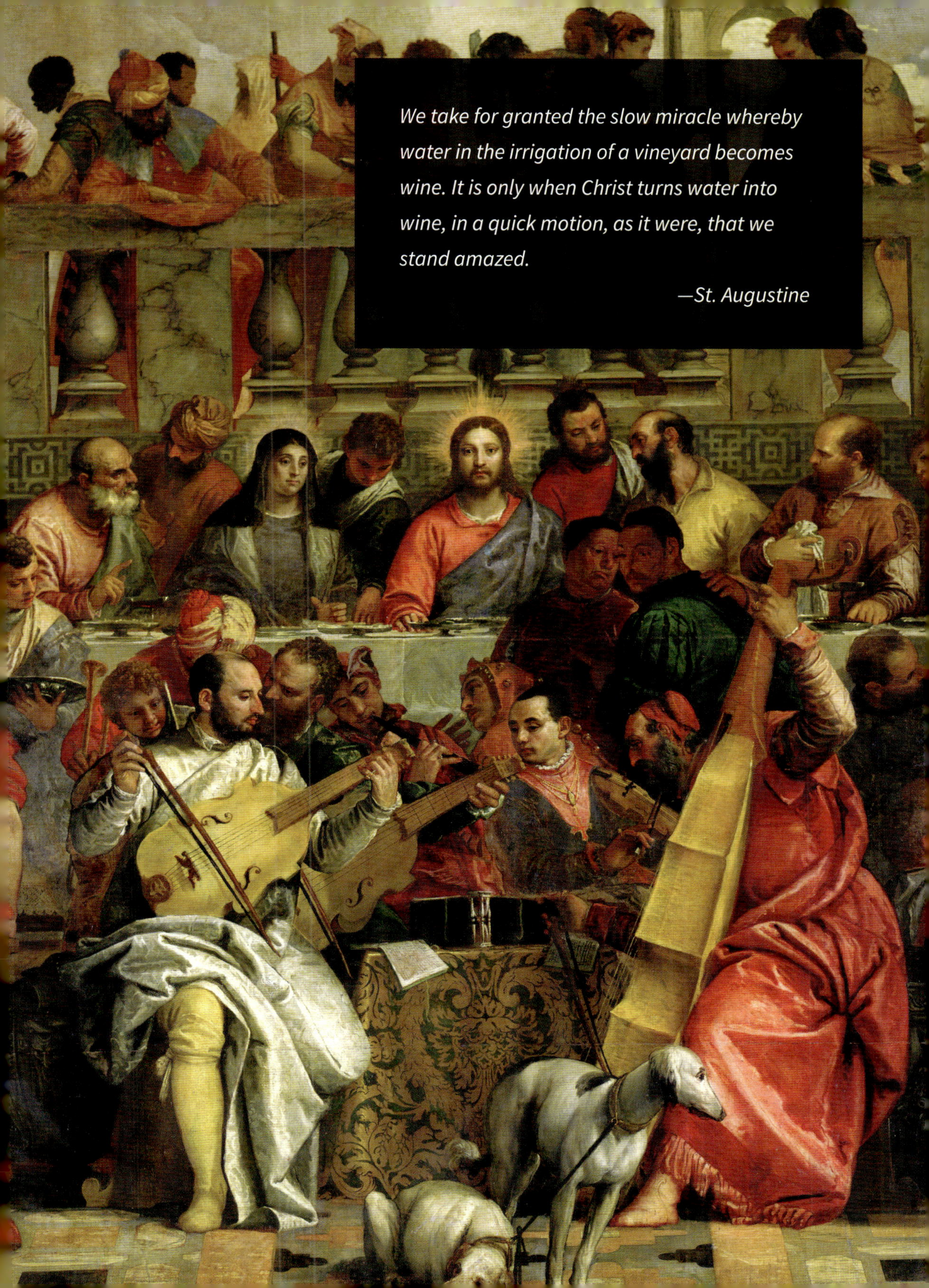

We take for granted the slow miracle whereby water in the irrigation of a vineyard becomes wine. It is only when Christ turns water into wine, in a quick motion, as it were, that we stand amazed.

—St. Augustine

A SHORT PRAYER

Mother of Mercy, pray for us.

FOR ME TO REMEMBER

1. Jesus changed water into wine at the wedding feast in Cana.
2. This was the first miracle that Jesus worked.
3. Mary is always ready to help you, too, if you ask her.

FOR ME TO DO

1. Write a little prayer telling Mary you will do everything to please her.
2. Draw a picture of one of the water pots. Color it with bright colors.
3. Dramatize this story for your friends.
4. Consider how you can help others who need help, as Jesus did.

LESSON 36

The Loaves and Fishes

Wherever Jesus went, large crowds of people followed Him. They listened to everything that He said. They asked Him to help them. They brought the sick and the crippled to Him. The people loved to be near Jesus.

Once when it was late afternoon and the people were still with our Lord, the Apostles wanted to send them home. But Jesus knew that everyone was tired and hungry. He could not

send them home. Jesus asked if anyone had food with them. Andrew found a young boy with five loaves of bread and two little fishes.

Jesus told everyone to sit down on the grass. Then He called the boy. Jesus blessed the bread and fishes and told the Apostles to give the food to the people.

There were five thousand men, besides all the women and children in the crowd. But the Apostles had more than enough food for everyone.

After all the people had eaten, Jesus told the Apostles to gather up all the food that was not eaten. The Apostles gathered up twelve baskets of food that had been left over.

When the people saw this great miracle, they wanted to make Jesus their king. Jesus knew what they were thinking, so He disappeared. He went up to a mountain to pray to His heavenly Father.

This miracle of bread and fishes was one of our Lord's greatest miracles. But every day at Mass, Jesus works a greater miracle with bread. He changes bread and wine into His own body and blood. Every day He gives us food for our bodies too.

A SHORT PRAYER

Hail, true Body born of Mary the Virgin.

FOR ME TO REMEMBER

1. Jesus fed five thousand people with five loaves of bread and two fishes.
2. This was one of our Lord's greatest miracles.

FOR ME TO DO

1. Draw a picture of the multiplication of the loaves and fishes.
2. Read stories about some of the miracles of Jesus.

LESSON 37

Palm Sunday

After Jesus had worked many miracles and taught the people for about three years He was ready to do His greatest work on earth. He was about to offer Himself to God as a sacrifice for us.

Jesus called His twelve Apostles to Him. He said that it was time to go to Jerusalem. It was time for the great feast of the Passover.

Do you know why the Jews celebrate the feast of the Passover? It was a remembrance of the time when God freed them from slavery in Egypt.

On the way to Jerusalem Jesus told the Apostles all the things that would happen to Him while He was there, but the Apostles did not understand any of the things that Jesus told them.

The Apostles got a donkey and Jesus rode on it into Jerusalem. When the people saw Him coming, they spread their garments on the road, waved palm branches in the air, and shouted out with joy: "Hosanna! Blessed is he who comes in the name of the Lord."

The enemies of Jesus did not like this, so they planned to kill Him.

A SHORT PRAYER

Blessed is he who comes in the name of the Lord; Hosanna in the highest.

FOR ME TO REMEMBER

1. Jesus rode into Jerusalem on Palm Sunday.
2. Great crowds of people welcomed Him.
3. They sang, "Hosanna! Blessed is he who comes in the name of the Lord."

FOR ME TO DO

1. Write a three sentence story telling how the Church celebrates Palm Sunday every year.
2. Memorize the words that the people sang when Jesus came into Jerusalem. See if you can find them in the words of the Mass.

LESSON 38

Holy Thursday

On Holy Thursday evening, Jesus and His Apostles ate the Last Supper. Jesus looked at His Apostles and said, "I have greatly desired to eat this Passover with you before I suffer."

Before He ate, Jesus washed the feet of His Apostles. He said, "As I have done to you, so you also should do."

Then He said, "Now you are clean, but not all." Jesus said this because He knew that Judas was going to betray Him. Judas was

planning to sell Jesus to His enemies that night for thirty pieces of silver.

Jesus was sad. He said to Judas, "What you plan to do, do quickly." Then Judas rose and left the room. He went out into the night to find the men who promised him the thirty pieces of silver for betraying Jesus to them.

Now a very holy moment had come. Jesus took bread and gave thanks to God. He blessed and broke the bread and gave it to His Apostles saying, "Take and eat; this is My Body."

Then Jesus took a cup of wine, blessed it, and gave it to His Apostles saying, "All of you drink of this; for this is My Blood which is being shed for many for the forgiveness of sins."

Then He said to His Apostles, "Do this in remembrance of Me."

Jesus had just said the first Mass. Jesus had given the promised gift of Himself, the Holy Eucharist, to the world. Jesus had just made His Apostles the first priests. What a holy night that was! Solemn, too. The next day Jesus was to die.

"Do this in remembrance of Me."

A SHORT PRAYER

Jesus, Savior of the world, sanctify Thy priests and sacred ministers.

FOR ME TO REMEMBER

1. Jesus said the first Mass on Holy Thursday night.
2. On the night before He died, Jesus gave us the sacrament of the Holy Eucharist.
3. Jesus made the Apostles His first priests.

FOR ME TO DO

1. Visit Jesus in the Blessed Sacrament often, especially during Holy Week.
2. Read the Bible story of the Last Supper.
3. Receive our Lord often if you can.
4. On Holy Thursday, pray for priests.

LESSON 39

Jesus Offers Himself for Us on the Cross—Good Friday

On Friday morning, Jesus was taken to Pontius Pilate, the Roman governor. Our Lord's enemies stood outside the governor's palace and shouted that Jesus was bad, and that He should be crucified.

As soon as Pilate spoke to Jesus, he saw that Jesus was not a bad man. He tried to save Jesus from being crucified by having his soldiers scourge Him. He thought that when the people saw that Jesus had been scourged, they would not want to crucify Him. Then he could let Jesus go free. So the soldiers took Jesus and beat Him with whips.

Because Jesus said He was a king, a purple cloak was put on Him, a crown of thorns was placed on His head, and a reed put in His hand. Then the soldiers made fun of Him, saying, "Hail, King of the Jews!" They spat on Him, and took the reed and kept striking Him on the head.

Jesus suffered all this without saying a word. Then He was taken back to Pontius Pilate. He took Jesus before the people and said, "Behold, the Man!"

But the people shouted, "Crucify Him! Crucify Him!"

Pontius Pilate did not want to see Jesus put to death, but the people cried out that if Pilate released Jesus, he would be no friend of Caesar. They said that everyone who makes himself King sets himself against Caesar. So Pilate told the Jews to take Jesus away and crucify Him.

Jesus was given a heavy cross. He had to carry it to a hill outside the city. This hill was called Mount Calvary.

Cruel soldiers nailed Jesus to the cross. His blood flowed from His wounds onto the ground.

Jesus was not angry with His enemies. Instead, He prayed for them. He said, "Father, forgive them, for they do not know what they are doing."

Jesus suffered very much while He hung on the cross. Mary, John the Apostle, and a few holy women were near the cross, but they could not help Jesus. He had to suffer alone.

After three long hours of suffering, Jesus bowed His head and died. The death of Jesus on the cross was a sacrifice to God. Jesus was the priest who offered the sacrifice. Jesus was also the victim that was offered to God. The cross was the altar on which Jesus offered Himself as a victim to God.

Jesus offered His sufferings and death to God to satisfy, that is, make up for our sins. That is why He is called the Redeemer. This work of redeeming us is called the Redemption. *By the Redemption is meant that Jesus Christ offered His sufferings and death to God in satisfaction for the sins of men.*

Why did Jesus offer Himself as a sacrifice to God? First, He offered Himself to adore God for us. Second, He offered Himself to thank God for all His favors to us. Third, He offered Himself to God to make up for our sins. Fourth, He offered Himself to ask God's blessings and favors for all men.

What do we learn from the sufferings and death of Christ? *From the sufferings and death of Christ we learn God's love for man and the evil of sin.*

After Jesus died, one of His friends went to Pilate and asked to take Jesus down from the cross. The body of Jesus was taken down from the cross and laid in His Mother's arms. Then it was wrapped in a linen cloth and placed in the tomb. A large stone was then rolled before the door of the tomb and soldiers were sent to guard it.

While the body of Jesus was in the tomb, where was His soul? When we say the "Apostles' Creed" we say that Jesus descended into hell. What does that mean? *When we say that*

Christ descended into hell we mean that, after He died, the soul of Christ descended into a place or state of rest, called limbo, where the souls of the just were waiting for Him. They were waiting for Him to reopen the gates of heaven.

Greater love has no man that this, that a man lay down his life for his friends.

—John 15:13

A SHORT PRAYER

Hail, O cross, our only hope.

FOR ME TO REVIEW

Catechism Lesson

83. **Q. Why did Christ suffer and die?**
A. Christ suffered and died for our sins.

84. **Q. What lessons do we learn from the sufferings and death of Christ?**
A. From the sufferings and death of Christ we learn the great evil of sin, the hatred God bears to it, and the necessity of satisfying for it.

85. **Q. Whither did Christ's soul go after His death?**
A. After Christ's death His soul descended into hell.

86. **Q. Did Christ's soul descend into the hell of the damned?**
A. The hell into which Christ's soul descended was not the hell of the damned, but a place or state of rest called limbo, where the souls of the just were waiting for Him.

FOR ME TO REMEMBER

1. Jesus died for our sins on Good Friday.
2. Jesus was crucified on Mount Calvary.
3. By His sufferings and death, Jesus reopened to us the gates of heaven.
4. By His sufferings and death, Jesus earned grace for us.
5. We call the sufferings and death of Jesus on the cross the Redemption.

6. After Jesus died, His soul went to limbo.
7. No one would ever do for me what Jesus has done for me.

FOR ME TO DO

1. Learn the prayer, "Act of Hope."
2. Follow Jesus on His journey to Calvary by making the Stations of the Cross every day during Lent.

LESSON 40

Jesus Offers Himself in the Mass

We know that Jesus suffered very much when He died on the cross. He wanted to give His life to God for us. That was the biggest sacrifice that He could make.

After Jesus died, He did not want His sacrifice of the cross to stop. He wanted to offer Himself to God for us over and over again. Jesus could not die again, but He could offer Himself to God as often as He wished. That is why He gave us the Mass. The Mass is a sacrifice. It is the same sacrifice as the sacrifice of the cross. Let us see why.

In the sacrifice of the cross, Jesus was the Priest. He offered Himself to God. In the sacrifice of the Mass the priest whom we see at the altar is taking the place of Jesus. So we say that in the Mass, too, Jesus is the priest who offers Himself to God. Jesus was also the victim offered to God on the cross. The victim and the priest are the same in each. So the sacrifice is the same.

On the cross Jesus shed His blood. That is why we say that the sacrifice of the cross was a bloody sacrifice.

In the Mass, Jesus does not shed His blood. That is why we say that the sacrifice of the Mass is an unbloody sacrifice.

In every Mass, Jesus offers Himself as He did on the cross: first, to adore God for us; second, to thank God for His favors; third, to make up for our sins; fourth, to ask God for the favors we want.

The Mass has three very important parts. The first important part of the Mass is the Offertory in which the priest offers bread and wine to God. He asks God to be pleased with our gift. God wants us to take part in the Mass. At the Offertory we can please God by joining Jesus in offering ourselves to Him.

The second important part of the Mass is the Consecration. Here the priest does what Christ told him to do. He changes the bread and wine into Christ's body and blood.

The third important part of the Mass is the Communion. Here the priest receives the body and blood of Jesus Christ. After he receives our Lord, the priest goes to the altar rail to give Holy Communion to the people. Let us try to receive Communion often. Even when we are not able to receive we can still invite Jesus into our hearts and talk to Him as we do after Communion.

Love the Mass. It is the holiest act that man can offer to God.

A SHORT PRAYER

My Lord and my God!

FOR ME TO REMEMBER

1. The sacrifice of the Mass is the same sacrifice as that of the cross.
2. Every day Jesus offers Himself to God in the Mass.
3. The Mass has three important parts: the Offertory, the Consecration, and the Communion.
4. The Mass is the greatest sacrifice that can he offered to God.

FOR ME TO DO

1. Attend Mass as often as you can.
2. Offer yourself to God each time you go to Mass.
3. Say the prayer, "My Lord and my God," at the Elevation of the Mass.

LESSON 41

Jesus Rises From the Dead

On Easter Sunday morning the holy women went to the tomb of Jesus. As they walked along they said to one another, "Who will roll the stone back from the entrance of the tomb for us?" It was very large. When they arrived at the tomb they saw that the stone had been rolled back.

The women entered the tomb. They did not find the body of the Lord Jesus. They saw an angel, and the angel said to them, "Do not be afraid; for I know that you seek Jesus, who was crucified. He is not here, for He has risen even as He said. Come, see the place where the Lord was laid. And go quickly and tell His Apostles that He has risen."

"O Death, where is your sting? O Hell, where is your victory? Christ is risen, and you are overthrown. Christ is risen, and the demons are fallen. Christ is risen, and the angels rejoice. Christ is risen, and life reigns. Christ is risen, and not one dead remains in the grave. For Christ, being risen from the dead, is become the first fruits of those who have fallen asleep. To Him be glory and dominion unto ages of ages."

—ST. JOHN CHRYSOSTOM

When the Apostles heard the news that Jesus had risen from the dead, Peter and John ran to the grave. The tomb was empty. Where was Jesus?

Later in the day, Jesus appeared to some of His friends. Then they believed that Jesus had risen from the dead.

How different the body of Jesus was after He had risen from the dead. Now He could not suffer. His body was glorious. Now His body was immortal. He could not die again. That is why we say that *Christ rose from the dead, glorious and immortal, on Easter Sunday, the third day after His death.*

Why did Jesus rise from the dead? Jesus rose from the dead to prove that He is God and to show us that some day we, too, will rise from the dead. Our bodies will be glorious and immortal. Our bodies and souls will live with God forever in heaven.

A SHORT PRAYER

Pray for us, O Holy Mother of God, that we may be made worthy of the promises of Christ.

FOR ME TO REVIEW

Catechism Lesson

89. **Q. On what day did Christ rise from the dead?**
A. Christ rose from the dead, glorious and immortal, on Easter Sunday, the third day after His death.

FOR ME TO REMEMBER

1. Jesus rose from the dead on Easter Sunday.
2. By His resurrection, He proved that He is God.
3. Like Jesus, our bodies, too, will rise from the dead.

FOR ME TO DO

1. Draw a picture of the Easter story.
2. Read the Easter story from the Bible..
3. In the Mass, at the Offertory, offer yourself to God as Jesus does.

LESSON 42

Jesus Ascends Into Heaven

After Jesus rose from the dead, He wanted the Catholic Church to continue His work. He had need of good and holy leaders for this work, so He made the Apostles His first bishops and Peter the first pope. It was during this time that Jesus told the Apostles much about His Church and what it should teach. Jesus did this because the Apostles were going to continue the work that He had started.

On the fortieth day after Easter, while Jesus and His Apostles were on a high mountain, Jesus said to them, "Go into the whole world and preach the gospel to every creature. He who believes and is baptized shall be saved, but he who does not believe shall be condemned."

Jesus also told them that they should stay in Jerusalem until He would send the Holy Spirit to them.

After Jesus had said these things "He lifted up His hands and blessed them. And it came to pass as He blessed them, that He parted from them and was carried up into heaven."

Christ ascended, body and soul, into heaven on Ascension Day, forty days after His Resurrection.

Now Jesus is in heaven. He is God. He is all-wise, all-powerful, all-good, and all-holy. He is equal to the Father and the Holy Spirit in all things. Jesus is man, too. As man, He has the highest

place in heaven. We say that He sits at the right hand of God, the Father Almighty.

When we say that Christ sits at the right hand of God, the Father Almighty, we mean that our Lord as God is equal to the Father, and that as man He has the highest place in heaven, next to God.

At the end of the world, He will come to judge the living and the dead. What does that mean? *When we say that Christ will come from thence to judge the living and the dead, we mean that on the last day our Lord will come to judge everyone who has ever lived in this world.*

Later on in this book, we will find out how Jesus will judge everybody who ever lived in this world.

A SHORT PRAYER

Christ, have mercy on us.

FOR ME TO REVIEW

Catechism Lesson

90. Q. **How long did Christ stay on earth after His resurrection?**
    A. Christ stayed on earth forty days after His resurrection to show that He was truly risen from the dead, and to instruct His Apostles.

91. Q. **After Christ had remained forty days on earth whither did He go?**
    A. After forty days Christ ascended into heaven, and the day on which He ascended into heaven is called Ascension day.

92. Q. **Where is Christ in heaven?**
    A. In heaven Christ sits at the right hand of God the Father Almighty.

93. Q. **What do you mean by saying that Christ sits at the right hand of God?**
    A. When I say that Christ sits at the right hand of God I mean that Christ as God is equal to His Father in all things, and that as man He is in the highest place in heaven next to God.

Questions

1. What thoughts come to your mind when you look at a crucifix?
2. On Holy Thursday, how can you especially show that you appreciate the sacrament of Holy Eucharist?

3. Why should boys and girls make the Way of the Cross?
4. Why do we call Jesus our Redeemer?
5. Why were the souls in limbo happy on Good Friday?
6. How does the story of Good Friday show us the evil of sin?

FOR ME TO REMEMBER

1. Jesus went to heaven on Ascension Day, forty days after He rose from the dead.
2. Jesus will come at the end of the world to judge the living and the dead.

FOR ME TO DO

1. Memorize the words that Jesus said to the Apostles just before He ascended into heaven.

Write your answers on a separate sheet of paper

Part 1 Short Answer

1. How old was Jesus when He began to teach the people?
2. Who "baptized" Jesus?
3. Why did the devil tempt Jesus?
4. What was the first miracle of Jesus?
5. Why did Jesus perform miracles?
6. Where did the first Palm Sunday procession take place?
7. When was the Last Supper?
8. What great powers did the Apostles receive at the Last Supper?
9. When did Jesus give us the sacrament of the Holy Eucharist?
10. When did Jesus say the first Mass?
11. Where did Jesus die?
12. On what day did Jesus die?
13. Why did Jesus die?
14. Why was the death of Jesus a sacrifice?
15. How long was the body of Jesus in the tomb?
16. Where was the soul of Jesus while His body was in the tomb?
17. What is the Mass?
18. What are the three important parts of the Mass?
19. Why is the Mass the greatest sacrifice?
20. Is the sacrifice of the Mass the same as the sacrifice of the cross?
21. When did Jesus rise from the dead?

22. When did Jesus go back to heaven?

23. When will Jesus come to judge the living and the dead?

Part 2 Completion

Write 1 to 8 on another paper. Find the correct word for each sentence from the list.

Holy Thursday	Good Friday	Holy Eucharist
Easter Sunday	Last Supper	Penance
Ascension Day	Apostles	
Calvary	Palm Sunday	

1. Jesus rose from the dead on ______.
2. Jesus was welcomed into Jerusalem on ______.
3. On Holy Thursday night Jesus gave us the sacrament of ______.
4. The name of the hill on which Jesus died was ______.
5. The day on which Jesus died was ______.
6. Jesus went to heaven on ______.
7. The ______ were made priests on Holy Thursday night.
8. Jesus said the first Mass at the ______.

Part 3

Show your two best reasons for loving to hear Mass.

A. You can watch the priest and the altar boy.

B. You can join the priest in offering Jesus to God.

C. You can learn to use your prayer book.

D. You can join your offering with the offering of Jesus.

Part 4 Yes or No

On another paper write 1 to 6 and answer each question with yes or no.

1. Did Jesus make up for everyone's sins when He died?
2. Can you join the priest at Mass in offering Jesus to God?
3. Could we ourselves ever entirely make up to God for our sins?
4. Will receiving Holy Communion help you take a greater part in the Mass?
5. Has anyone besides Jesus ever risen from the dead by his own power?
6. Is the Mass a sacrifice?

Part 5 Multiple Choice

Answer 1 to 4 on your own paper as you did before with A or B or C.

1. The day on which Jesus proved that He is God was:
   A. Christmas.
   B. Easter.
   C. Pentecost.
2. Jesus was condemned to death by:
   A. Pilate.
   B. Herod.
   C. Annas.

3. The part of the Mass at which we should make an offering of ourselves to God is:
   A. the Consecration.
   B. the Communion.
   C. the Offertory.

4. Jesus will come to judge the living and the dead on:
   A. Christmas.
   B. New Year's.
   C. the last day of the world.

UNIT

3 I Believe in the Holy Spirit and the Holy Catholic Church

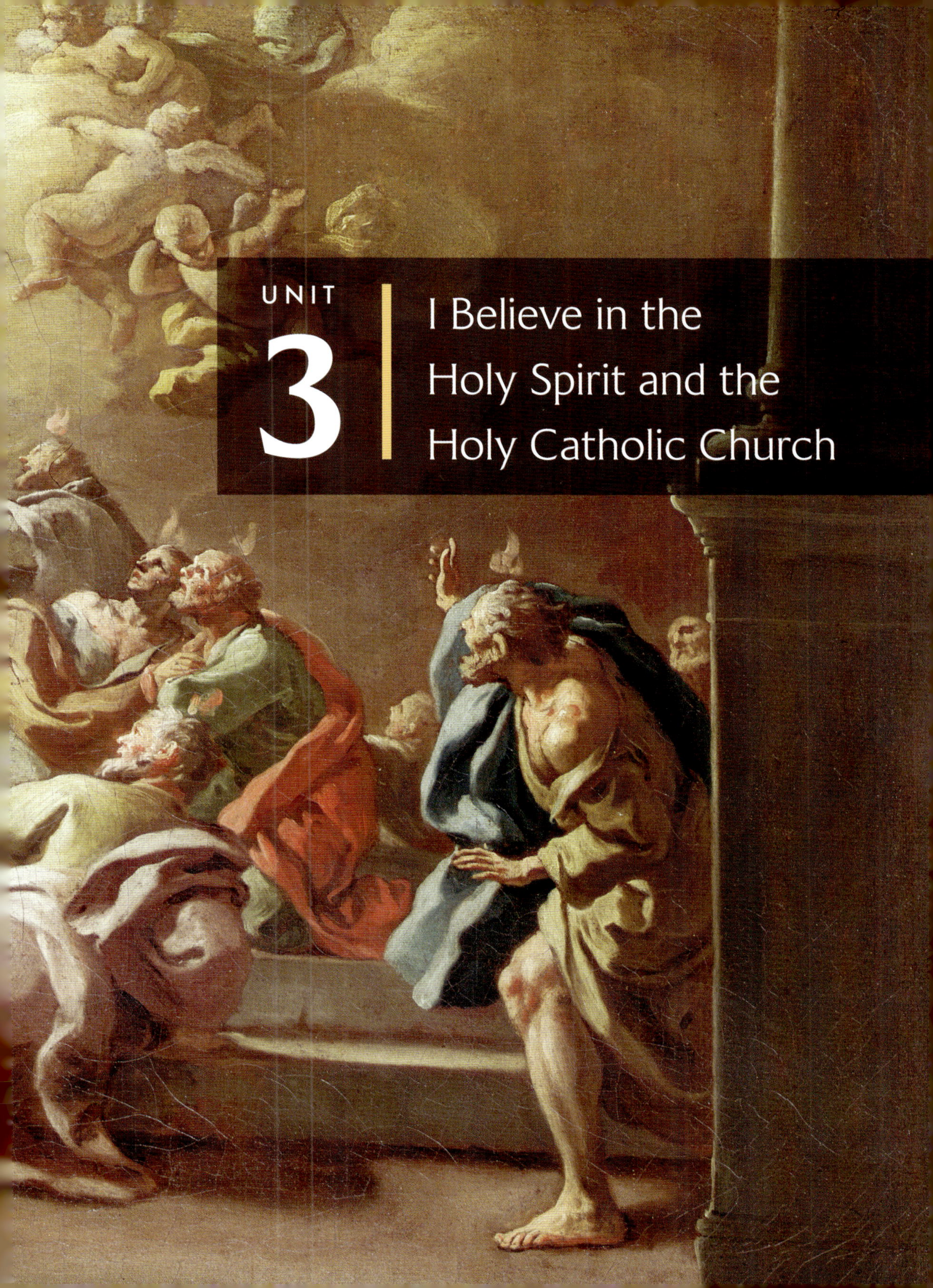

CHAPTER 5

God the Holy Spirit Comes to Do His Work

LESSON 43

Jesus Sends the Holy Spirit

It was the tenth day after Jesus ascended into heaven. The Apostles, the Blessed Virgin Mary, and the other disciples were in the Upper Room. It was the same room where Jesus had eaten the Last Supper with His Apostles.

They had spent ten days in prayer, for they were getting their hearts ready for the coming of the Holy Spirit. *The Holy Spirit is God and the third Person of the Blessed Trinity,* whom Jesus had promised to send to them.

All at once they heard a loud sound from heaven. It was like a great wind and it filled the whole room where they were sitting. Little tongues of fire rested over the heads of each one present in the room. The Holy Spirit came into the souls of Mary, the Apostles, and the disciples. He filled them with wisdom and strength. They were no longer afraid of the enemies of Jesus. They went out and talked to the people about Him. Peter talked to many people about Jesus. They listened and believed all that Peter said. They begged Peter to baptize them, and on that day he baptized about three thousand people.

Jesus sent the Holy Spirit to be with the Church right from its beginning. The Holy Spirit guards and guides the Catholic Church and will do so until the end of the world. This is why the Catholic Church will last until the end of the world.

The Apostles worked for many years telling people about Jesus and His Church. Before they died they appointed others to

take their place. They obeyed our Lord's command when He said, "Go into the whole world and preach the gospel to every creature." Today priests of the Catholic Church go to all countries of the world to tell people about Jesus and His Church.

A SHORT PRAYER

O Mary, Queen of the clergy, pray for us; obtain for us many and holy priests.

FOR ME TO REVIEW

Catechism Lesson

94. Q. Who is the Holy Spirit?

A. The Holy Spirit is the third Person of the Blessed Trinity.

FOR ME TO REMEMBER

1. The Holy Spirit came down upon the Apostles ten days after Jesus went back to heaven.
2. The Holy Spirit came in the form of tongues of fire.
3. Pentecost is the day on which the Holy Spirit came down upon the Apostles.
4. The Holy Spirit will stay with the Church until the end of the world.

FOR ME TO DO

1. Draw a picture of the Apostles and the Blessed Virgin in the Upper Room, when the Holy Spirit came upon them.
2. Make up a little play showing how the Apostles acted before and after the Holy Spirit came.
3. Say the Sign of the Cross and the "Glory be . . ." with devotion, in honor of the Holy Spirit.

LESSON 44

The Holy Spirit Gives Us Grace

The Holy Spirit lives in the soul of every person in the state of sanctifying grace. He watches over us every minute of the day. He gives us grace when we need it.

What important work does the Holy Spirit do for souls in which He lives? *The Holy Spirit sanctifies souls through the gift of grace.* This means He makes souls holy with His grace.

What is grace? Grace is a gift from God. When we receive something free from someone we call it a gift, a present. Every day we get gifts from God. We get God's help. He makes us holy. He helps us to be good. We call it God's grace. We also call it a supernatural gift. We do not earn God's grace. It is a free gift from Him to help us get to heaven.

When Jesus died on the cross He earned many graces for us. Every day we can receive some of these graces that Jesus earned when He died for us.

There are two kinds of grace: sanctifying grace and actual grace. We will learn about these two kinds of grace in the next lesson.

Those whose hearts are pure are temples of the Holy Spirit.

—St. Lucy

A SHORT PRAYER

God the Holy Spirit, have mercy on us.

FOR ME TO REVIEW

Catechism Lesson

100. Q. Why did Christ send the Holy Spirit?

A. Christ sent the Holy Spirit to sanctify His Church, to enlighten and strengthen the Apostles, and to enable them to preach the Gospel.

104. Q. How many kinds of grace are there?

A. There are two kinds of grace—sanctifying grace and actual grace.

FOR ME TO REMEMBER

1. The Holy Spirit gives us grace.
2. Grace is a supernatural gift from God.
3. There are two kinds of grace: sanctifying grace and actual grace.

FOR ME TO DO

1. As soon as you awaken in the morning, ask Jesus to help you to make good use of all the graces He will send you this day.

LESSON 45

The Holy Spirit Makes Us Holy—Sanctifying grace

What is sanctifying grace? Sanctifying grace is a supernatural gift from God which does many wonderful things to us.

God gave us our natural life. God also gave us natural gifts. Do you know what our natural gifts are? They are our eyes and ears, our hands and feet, our minds and hearts, our bodies and our souls. With our natural life and gifts, we are able to live on this earth. God has also made it possible for us to have supernatural life. This supernatural life is a sharing of the life of God by the soul. This is what we mean when we say the soul is in the state of sanctifying grace. To sanctify means to make holy. This grace, therefore, makes the soul holy and pleasing to God.

Let us see what *sanctifying grace* does for us. *First,* sanctifying grace *makes us holy and pleasing to God.* When our souls are filled with grace they are holy. God is pleased with them.

Second, sanctifying grace *makes us adopted children of God.* When we were born we were not holy and pleasing to God. But on the day we were baptized, God came to live in our souls with His sanctifying grace. We became His adopted children. We became brothers and sisters of Christ. How wonderful!

Third, sanctifying grace *makes us temples of the Holy Spirit.* On the day that we were baptized, the Holy Spirit came to live in our souls. He loves us so much that He wants to live in us. If we remember that the Holy Spirit is living in us, will we ever want to offend God by sin?

Fourth, sanctifying grace *enables us to live with God on earth and for eternity in heaven.* Have you ever tried some of your parents' coffee? Upon a first sip, you may consider coffee to be bitter and distasteful. Often, it is only after drinking many cups of coffee over the course of weeks, months, or even years that you begin to acquire a taste for it. C. S. Lewis once called Heaven an "acquired taste" because the happiness we experience there is only enjoyed by those who have lived in God's sanctifying grace. Sanctifying grace enables our souls to enjoy living with God in heaven. When our souls do not have sanctifying grace, heaven and the things of God are distasteful and even painful to us. To have sanctifying grace in the soul is to already live with and enjoy the goodness of God.

When we die with sanctifying grace in our souls, we will continue to enjoy the goodness of God for all eternity in heaven. We must have sanctifying grace to enter heaven.

Sanctifying grace not only makes us pleasing to God, but it also makes our actions supernatural. Supernatural actions are pleasing to God, and are even more so when they are performed with the intention to love and praise God by them. Walking to school every day is a natural act. You use your legs and feet, which are natural gifts, to get to school. This simple act can be turned into a supernatural act if you have the right disposition and intention. Actions performed for the love of God please God very much, and they increase our ability to enjoy God in heaven––this is called *merit*. Our actions can gain merit for heaven when they are performed in the state of grace and done for the love of God. Every time you do an act that gains merit, God the Holy Spirit puts

> *Sanctifying grace is an habitual gift, a stable and supernatural disposition that perfects the soul itself to enable it to live with God, to act by his love.*
>
> *—Catechism of the Catholic Church, 2000*

more sanctifying grace into your soul. This grace makes your soul grow more holy and pleasing to God.

Can we ever lose sanctifying grace? Yes, all sanctifying grace will leave our soul if we commit a mortal sin. With sanctifying grace gone from our souls we are not holy. We are not pleasing to God. We are no longer His friends. We have shut out the Holy Spirit from our souls. We are no longer temples of the Holy Spirit. We no longer are able to enjoy the goodness of God on earth or in heaven.

Will God give sanctifying grace back to us after we lose it by mortal sin? Yes, God continues to be a loving and merciful Father. He still gives us His help. If we are sorry and receive the sacrament of Penance and Reconciliation worthily, God will give back to us the sanctifying grace that we lost through mortal sin. We will again be holy and pleasing to God.

A SHORT PRAYER

May the grace of the Holy Spirit enlighten our senses and our hearts.

FOR ME TO REVIEW

Catechism Lesson

105. Q. What is sanctifying grace?

A. Sanctifying grace is that grace which makes the soul holy and pleasing to God.

FOR ME TO REMEMBER

1. Sanctifying grace makes our souls holy and pleasing to God.
2. Sanctifying grace makes us God's children.

3. Sanctifying grace makes us temples of the Holy Spirit.
4. Sanctifying grace enables us to live with God on earth and in heaven.

FOR ME TO DO

1. Say a Morning Offering each day so that all your actions are turned over to God for Him to use and make meritorious.
2. Treat others as children of God. Serve them by doing the works of mercy.

LESSON 46

Actual Grace

What is actual grace? *Actual grace is a supernatural help of God which enlightens our mind and strengthens our will to do good and avoid evil.* Actual grace helps us see what is right and makes us eager to do it. Actual grace makes our acts holy.

Sometimes it is hard for us to know the right thing to do. God the Holy Spirit enlightens our minds with actual grace. He shows us what is right.

Knowing what is right is not enough, even if we are eager to do it. We need help to do the right thing. Because of original sin, our wills lack the help that made them strong. So God gives us actual grace to make us brave enough to do good and stay away from sin.

We know that it is a sin to tell a lie. It is easy to tell lies and it is often hard to tell the truth. We need actual grace to make us want to tell the truth, to strengthen our wills to tell the truth, and to keep from telling a lie. We must try to make use of all the actual grace that God gives us.

If we do not use God's actual grace and thereby lose His help we will not be able to do good and stay away from sin.

Jesus died so that all of us might go to heaven with Him when we die. God wants us to be good. That is why the Holy Spirit offers us the help of actual grace all during life.

A SHORT PRAYER

O God, come to my assistance. O Lord, make haste to help me.

FOR ME TO REVIEW

Catechism Lesson

110. Q. What is actual grace?

A. Actual grace is that help of God which enlightens our mind and moves our will to shun evil and do good.

FOR ME TO REMEMBER

1. God gives us actual grace.
2. God gives us all the help we need every day.
3. We should make good use of the graces God gives us each day.

FOR ME TO DO

1. Make a list of the ways by which you can use God's grace today.

LESSON 47

How We Obtain Grace

In order to enter heaven we need grace. God gave us two special ways to get the grace we need. *The principal ways of obtaining grace are prayer and the sacraments, especially the Holy Eucharist.*

Every time we pray, God puts grace into our souls. Every time we offer all our thoughts, words, and actions as a prayer to God during the day, He gives us grace.

But prayer is not the only way to get grace. We can also get grace by receiving the sacraments. The names of the seven sacraments are Baptism, Confirmation, Holy Eucharist, Penance and Reconciliation, Anointing of the Sick, Holy Orders, and Matrimony. These seven sacraments are Jesus' gift of love to us. They are the ways in which grace and salvation come to us. In the sacraments Jesus gives us His hand to hold and the merits of His death on the cross to use as we walk through life with all its trials and temptations.

How much grace does God want to give us? God's grace is always available to those who desire it and are open to receiving it. We should be open to all of the graces God wishes to give us so as to accomplish His will in the world and thereby increase our happiness with Him in heaven forever.

> *God opposes the proud, but gives grace to the humble.*
>
> *—James 4:6*

A SHORT PRAYER

O Jesus, with all my heart I cling to Thee.

FOR ME TO REVIEW

Catechism Lesson

114. Q. Which are the means instituted by our Lord to enable men at all times to share in the fruits of the Redemption?

A. The means instituted by our Lord to enable men at all times to share in the fruits of His Redemption are the Church and the sacraments.

FOR ME TO REMEMBER

1. Two big ways to obtain grace are prayer and the sacraments.
2. The seven sacraments are Baptism, Confirmation, Holy Eucharist, Penance and Reconciliation, Anointing of the Sick, Holy Orders, and Matrimony.

FOR ME TO DO

1. Offer your work as a prayer to God today.
2. Say the Morning Offering with devotion and love.
3. Memorize the names of the seven sacraments.

LESSON 48

The Theological Virtues and Gifts of the Holy Spirit

When the Holy Spirit came to us at Baptism, He made us holy and pleasing to God. He gave us the great gift of sanctifying grace and brought with His grace some other special powers. These powers make us able to live as good children of God.

The chief powers that are given to us with sanctifying grace are the three theological virtues and the seven gifts of the Holy Spirit.

"Theological" is a big word. It means that a thing has something to do with God. *The three theological virtues are faith, hope, and charity.* They are virtues which help us to believe in God, hope in God, and love God.

These gifts help us to know, love, and serve God better.

The seven gifts of the Holy Spirit were put into our souls at Baptism. They will be made stronger when we receive the sacrament of Confirmation.

The seven gifts of the Holy Spirit are:

- wisdom,
- understanding,
- counsel,
- fortitude,
- knowledge,
- piety,
- and fear of the Lord.

In what special way does each of these gifts help us to get to heaven?

A SHORT PRAYER

O God, make me a saint.

FOR ME TO REVIEW

Catechism Lesson

106. Q. What do you call those graces or gifts of God by which we believe in Him, hope in Him, and love Him?

A. Those graces or gifts of God by which we believe in Him, and hope in Him, and love Him, are called the theological virtues of faith, hope, and charity.

FOR ME TO REMEMBER

1. The chief powers that came to us at Baptism are the three theological virtues and the seven gifts of the Holy Spirit.
2. The three theological virtues are faith, hope, and charity.
3. The seven gifts of the Holy Spirit are wisdom, understanding, counsel, fortitude, knowledge, piety, and the fear of the Lord.

FOR ME TO DO

1. Learn the names of the theological virtues.
2. List ways to exercise each.
3. Practice writing the names of the seven gifts of the Holy Spirit to help you memorize them.
4. Learn a prayer to the Holy Spirit.

LESSON 49

Faith

Faith is one of the supernatural virtues. We received this virtue from God at Baptism. By this virtue of faith we believe all the truths taught to us by the Church about God. Our catechism tells us that *faith is the virtue by which we firmly believe on the word of God all the truths He has revealed.*

None of us has ever seen God. He is a spirit and cannot be seen with our eyes or touched with our hands. Faith teaches us to believe this truth that God is a pure spirit. The virtue of faith helps us to believe all the truths about God which Christ taught.

Must we believe everything that God has told us? Yes, we must believe all of God's truths even if we cannot understand them.

How do we practice the virtue of faith? We practice the virtue of faith by saying our prayers every day, by attending Holy Mass on Sundays and holy days of obligation, by receiving the sacraments often, and by learning our religion. Can you think of other ways?

When we practice the virtue of faith we really live our religion.

> *"Faith is to believe what you do not see; the reward of this faith is to see what you believe."*
>
> *—St. Augustine*

A SHORT PRAYER

Lord, increase our faith.

FOR ME TO REVIEW

Catechism Lesson

107. Q. What is faith?

A. Faith is a theological virtue by which we firmly believe the truths which God has revealed.

FOR ME TO REMEMBER

1. Faith is a virtue by which we believe all the truths God has revealed to us.
2. When we practice the virtue of faith we live our religion.

FOR ME TO DO

1. Practice writing the "Act of Faith."
2. Practice the virtue of faith by leading a good Catholic life.
3. Make a list of things you do every day which show that you believe in God.

LESSON 50

Hope

Hope is the good habit that makes us say, "I won't give up. God will help me save my soul."

We know that we cannot be perfectly happy here on this earth, because we were made for the happiness of heaven. We need God's help, plus our own cooperation to get there. We trust that we will get this help from God, because the Holy Spirit has put the virtue of hope into our souls.

What is hope? *Hope is the virtue by which we firmly trust that God will give us eternal happiness and the means to obtain it.*

God has promised eternal happiness to all those who know, love, and serve Him in this world. We know we are sinners, but we trust God to forgive us our sins, if we are sorry for them. We trust God to give us all the help we need to get to heaven.

Because hope is a virtue, it must be practiced so that it will grow strong within us. How do we practice the virtue of hope? We practice the virtue of hope by willingly doing what God wants us to do, and by cheerfully accepting the sorrows that He sends us. We practice hope by being patient when God sends us sickness or when death strikes around us.

God is our loving Father who knows our needs. He wants us to put our trust in Him. He knows what is best for each one of us. He wants us to feel sure that all things will turn out well if we place ourselves in His loving care.

A SHORT PRAYER

Heart of Jesus, I put my trust in Thee.

FOR ME TO REVIEW

Catechism Lesson

108. Q. What is hope?

A. Hope is a theological virtue by which we firmly trust that God will give us eternal life and the means to obtain it.

FOR ME TO REMEMBER

1. Hope is the virtue by which we trust that God will take us to heaven some day if we know, love, and serve Him in this world.

FOR ME TO DO

1. Practice writing the "Act of Hope" to help you memorize it correctly. Add it to your daily prayers.
2. Talk about how we show God we place our trust in Him.

LESSON 51

Charity

God loves us so much that He became man and died on the cross for us. God still shows His great love for us by giving us many wonderful gifts.

What does God want in return for His love? God wants us to love Him. Is that hard to do? No. God is so good, holy, and kind that it is easy to love Him.

Long before we knew anything about God, the virtue of love was put into our souls at Baptism. It was the Holy Spirit who gave us this supernatural virtue of love, which we call charity.

What is charity? *Charity is the virtue by which we love God above all things for His own sake, and our neighbor as ourselves for the love of God.*

How much does God want us to love Him? God wants us to love Him more than anything else in the world.

God is pleased when He hears us say, "Dear God, I love You," but He is more pleased when we show Him that we love Him. How can we do this?

We can show God that we truly love Him by practicing the virtue of charity.

We practice the virtue of charity every time we pray, every time we receive Jesus in Holy Communion, every time we do as God wants us to do. We show God we love Him when we keep His commandments. When we do these things our love for God grows stronger.

God also wants us to love our neighbor. God made him, too. He is God's child, just as we are. God wants us to love our neighbor as we love ourselves. God wants us to help our neighbor. If we love and help our neighbor because we love God, then we are not only showing that we love our neighbor, but we are also showing that we love God. Jesus said that whatever we do to others, we really do to Him.

Our faith will not be needed when we know God in heaven. Our hope for eternal happiness will end in the next world. But our love of God and our neighbor will go on in heaven for all eternity.

A SHORT PRAYER

Sacred Heart of Jesus, let me love Thee and make Thee loved.

FOR ME TO REVIEW

Catechism Lesson

109. Q. What is charity?

A. Charity is a theological virtue by which we love God above all things for His own sake, and our neighbor as ourselves for the love of God.

Questions

1. Mary wishes she could pray all day long to God. How can she do this?

2. Tell which phrases make you think of sanctifying grace and those which make you think of actual grace:
   a) Makes us holy temples.
   b) Prepares us to live in heaven.
   c) Makes us strong enough to say "no" to the devil.
   d) Helps us to know and do what is right.
   e) Makes our souls holy and pleasing to God.
   f) Puts good thoughts into our minds.
   g) Helps us to stay away from persons, places, or things that lead us into sin.
3. Which of these practices will help your faith grow stronger?
   a) Praying as often as you can.
   b) Reading good books.
   c) Studying and learning your religion lesson well.
   d) people that you know all that you ever have to know about your religion.

FOR ME TO REMEMBER

1. Charity is the virtue by which we love God above all things and our neighbor for the love of God.

FOR ME TO DO

1. Memorize the "Act of Love." Say it every day.
2. Draw pictures showing ways of practicing charity toward God and your neighbor.
3. Learn the prayer: My God, I love Thee.
4. Talk about things you can do to show your love of your neighbor. Then choose one each day, and do it.

Write your answers on a separate sheet of paper

Part 1 Short Answer

1. What is grace?
2. Who gives us grace?
3. How do we get grace?
4. What are the two kinds of grace?
5. What is sanctifying grace?
6. What does sanctifying grace do for our souls?
7. How do we lose sanctifying grace?
8. Can we get to heaven without sanctifying grace?
9. What is actual grace?
10. How do we get actual grace?
11. How do we lose actual grace?
12. Who gave us the seven sacraments?
13. What two sacraments can we receive often?
14. What are the theological virtues?

Part 2 Completion

Write 1 to 10 on another paper. Find the correct word for each sentence from the list.

purgatory	Holy Spirit	actual grace
Church	Jesus Christ	venial sin
mortal sin	sanctifying grace	penance
Pentecost	God	heaven

The third person of the Blessed Trinity is ______ (1).

The Apostles worked many years telling people about ______ (2) and His ______ (3).

The Holy Spirit lives in the soul of every person in the state of ______ (4).

Grace is a supernatural gift from ______ (5).

The two kinds of grace are ______ (6) and ______ (7).

Sanctifying grace makes us the temples of the ______ (8).

Sanctifying grace gives us a right to ______ (9).

God will give sanctifying grace back to us after we lose it by ______ (10).

Part 3 Yes or No

Write 1 to 5 on your own paper and answer each question with yes or no.

1. Sanctifying grace makes our soul holy and pleasing to God.
2. Actual grace helps us to do good and stay away from sin.
3. The seven gifts of the Holy Spirit were put into our souls when we made our first Holy Communion.
4. The three theological virtues are to know, love, and serve God.
5. The chief powers that came to us at Baptism are the three theological virtues and the seven gifts of the Holy Spirit.
6. Hope is the virtue by which we firmly believe all the truths that God has revealed.
7. Faith is the virtue by which we firmly trust in God.
8. We practice hope by being patient when God sends us sickness or death.
9. Charity is the virtue by which we love God above all things.

CHAPTER 6
The Work of the Holy Spirit in the Church

LESSON 52

The Holy Spirit and the Church

Our Lord sent the Holy Spirit to work in and through His Church.

When we speak of the Church, we do not mean a big building. We mean all the people all over the world who belong to the Church that Christ founded and all who are united with Christ in one big group or congregation of the faithful. These people have been baptized. They all accept the same true faith. This means that they believe the same holy truths which God has revealed. They have the same sacrifice of the Mass. They have the same seven sacraments. All these people are under the same head. They have the same leader. Their leader is our Holy Father, the pope.

Those members who fully belong to the Church we call Catholics. They belong to the Church which Jesus started. Our catechism teaches us that *the Church is the congregation of all baptized persons united in the same true faith, the same sacrifice, and the same sacraments, under the Holy Father, the pope.*

Why did Jesus Christ found the Church? *Jesus Christ founded the Church to bring all men to eternal salvation.* The Church is His kingdom on earth. Our Lord is the head of the Church. He unites us with Himself through His Church. He wants us to live in Him and through Him and for Him.

The Catholic Church is like a loving mother. That is why we call her Holy Mother Church. She knows what is best for us. If we listen to her teachings and use the helps she gives us to save our souls, we will safely find our way to heaven.

A SHORT PRAYER

Sacred Heart of Jesus, Thy kingdom come.

FOR ME TO REVIEW

Catechism Lesson

489. Q. What is the Church?

A. The Church is the congregation of all those who profess the faith of Christ, partake of the same sacraments, and are governed by their lawful pastors under one visible head, the pope.

508. Q. Why did Christ found the Church?

A. Christ founded the Church to teach, govern, sanctify, and save all men.

FOR ME TO REMEMBER

1. The Church is the congregation of all baptized persons who are united in the same true faith, in the same sacrifice, in the same sacraments, and under the same leader, the pope.
2. Jesus started the Church to bring all men to heaven.
3. We live in Jesus as members of His Church.

FOR ME TO DO

1. Make a list of some of the helps that the Catholic Church gives us to get to heaven.

LESSON 53

The Rulers of the Church

Jesus made the Apostles the first bishops or rulers of His Church. He gave them many powers in order to do this work for Him. He gave them the power to teach His truths to all people. He gave them the power to sanctify the members of His Church. Christ also gave His Apostles the power to make laws to guide the members of His Church.

To whom did Christ give the power to teach, to sanctify, and to rule the members of His Church? *Christ gave the power to teach, to sanctify, and to rule the members of His Church to the Apostles, the first bishops of the Church.*

Jesus Christ knew that the Apostles would not live forever on this earth. He also knew that they would not be able to baptize everyone in the whole world, or preach to everyone. Other helpers would be needed to do the work of the Apostles when they were dead. The Apostles were the first bishops. As bishops they had the power from Christ to pass on to other men their own great power to teach, sanctify, and to rule the members of the Church. This they did. *The successors of the Apostles are the bishops of the Church.* The bishops too can teach, sanctify, and rule the members of Christ's Church. Then they can give to priests powers like their own.

Jesus knew that the Apostles would need someone to rule and guide them in their work so *Christ gave special power in His Church to St. Peter by making him the head of the Apostles and chief teacher and ruler of the entire Church.*

Jesus Himself would always be the invisible head of the Church. He knew He would ascend into heaven. But here on earth, Peter would be the head, the visible head of the Church. He would take our Lord's place in ruling all the Catholics of the world. He would be the chief teacher of God's truths.

> And I tell you, you are Peter, and on this rock I will build my Church, and the gates of Hades shall not prevail against it.
>
> —Matthew 16:18

When St. Peter died, another holy man was chosen as pope. Since then many great popes have lived and died. Each one has been called a successor of St. Peter because he was bishop of Rome and has had the same powers as pope that Christ gave to St. Peter. Today, *the successor of St. Peter is the Holy Father, the bishop of Rome.* Do you know his name?

Our Holy Father, the pope, rules over millions of Catholics. He cannot do his work alone. He needs many helpers. The pope's helpers are called bishops.

The pope gives each bishop a certain number of Catholics to take care of. The bishop is to teach, sanctify, and rule these people. Do you know the name of your bishop?

The bishops have so much work to do that they also need some help in taking care of souls. Who helps the bishops with their work? *The priests, especially parish priests, help the bishops in the care of souls.*

What do the priests do? They offer Mass with the people. They give them the sacraments. They teach them God's truths. They help them to get to heaven.

The pope, the bishops, and the priests take our Lord's place here on earth. They are doing His work. Our Lord wants us to love, honor, and obey them always.

A SHORT PRAYER

Send forth, O Lord, laborers into Thy harvest.

FOR ME TO REVIEW

Catechism Lesson

525. Q. What do you mean by the authority of the Church?

A. By the authority of the Church I mean the right and power which the pope and the bishops, as the successors of the Apostles, have to teach and to govern the faithful.

499. Q. Why is the pope, the bishop of Rome, the visible head of the Church?

A. The pope, the bishop of Rome, is the visible head of the Church because he is the successor of St. Peter, whom Christ made the chief of the Apostles and the visible head of the Church.

507. Q. How do we know that the bishops of the Church are the successors of the Apostles?

A. We know that the bishops of the Church are the successors of the Apostles because they continue the work of the Apostles and give proof of the same authority. They have always exercised the rights and powers that belonged to the Apostles in making laws for the Church, in consecrating bishops and ordaining priests.

FOR ME TO REMEMBER

1. St. Peter was the first Pope.
2. The pope is the successor of St. Peter.
3. The pope is called the Holy Father, the bishop of Rome.
4. Jesus made the Apostles bishops.
5. The bishops are the successors of the Apostles.
6. The priests help the bishops with their work.

FOR ME TO DO

1. Draw or find pictures to show some of the things that the priests do for you. Talk about them.
2. Pray for the pope, the bishops, and the priests so they will do God's work well.

LESSON 54

The Marks of the Church

Jesus Christ started the Catholic Church. He wanted everyone in the world to belong to this Church. *The one true Church established by Christ is the Catholic Church.*

He wanted people to know that the Catholic Church is the true Church to which all must belong. So He gave His Church special signs, or marks, to help people know that the Catholic Church is the true Church. *We know that the Catholic Church is the one true Church established by Christ because it alone has the marks of the true Church.*

The marks of the Church are qualities of the Church which are like signs that point out to us that the Catholic Church is the only true Church. *The chief marks of the Church are four: It is one, holy, catholic or universal, and apostolic.* Let us see how these four marks show that the Catholic Church is the only true Church.

The Catholic Church is one. This means that all the people who belong to the Catholic Church believe the same holy truths, have the same sacrifice of the Mass, the same sacraments, and have the pope for their leader.

The Catholic Church is holy. Jesus Christ, the holiest Person who ever walked on this earth, started the Catholic Church. The Church was started to make us holy. It teaches us how to live a holy life. It gives us the seven sacraments to make us holy.

The Church is catholic or universal. This means that the Catholic Church is for all the people of every nation, race, or color. It also means that the Church will continue to teach the same holy truths to all men to the end of the world. Christ invites all *to belong to the Catholic Church, in some way, in order to be saved.*

The Four Marks of the Church

- One
- Holy
- Catholic (or Universal)
- Apostolic

The Church is apostolic. By this we mean that it was started by Christ and His Apostles. The powers that Christ gave to His Apostles to carry on the work of the Church were given to their successors. We have already learned that *the successors of the Apostles are the bishops of the Church.*

To express His desire for unity, Jesus said the following: "I am the good shepherd; and I know mine, and mine know me. As the Father knows me, and I know the Father: and I lay down my life for my sheep. And other sheep I have, that are not of this fold: them also I must bring, and they shall hear my voice, and there shall be one fold and one shepherd" (John 10:14–16). Many Catholics are not part of God's sheepfold because they do not live or believe in the truths of the faith. We must pray not only for non-Catholics, but for Catholics who have fallen away from Christ, the Good Shepherd.

A SHORT PRAYER

My God, make us to be of one mind in the truth and of one heart in charity.

FOR ME TO REVIEW

Catechism Lesson

548. Q. Has the Church any marks by which it may be known?

A. The Church has four marks by which it may be known: it is one; it is holy; it is catholic; it is apostolic.

509. Q. Are all bound to belong to the Church?

A. All are bound to belong to the Church, and he who knows the Church to be the true Church and remains out of it cannot be saved.

510. Q. Is it ever possible for one to be saved who does not know the Catholic Church to be the true Church?

A. It is possible for one to be saved who does not know the Catholic Church to be the true Church, provided that person: 1) has been validly baptized; 2) firmly believes the religion he professes and practices to be the true religion, and 3) dies without the guilt of mortal sin on his soul.

1125. Q. Is it enough to belong to God's Church in order to be saved?

A. It is not enough to belong to the Church in order to be saved, but we must also keep the commandments of God and of the Church.

FOR ME TO REMEMBER

1. The Catholic Church is the true Church started by Christ.
2. The Church has four chief marks to show that it is the true Church: It is one, holy, catholic or universal, and apostolic.

FOR ME TO DO

1. By your actions let everyone see that you are a worthy member of the holy Catholic Church.
2. Pray and work that all non-Catholics will become good and faithful Catholics, and that all Catholics my fully live and believe in the truths of the faith.
3. Talk about things you can do to share the truths of the Catholic faith with others.

LESSON 55

Communion of Saints—Forgiveness of Sins

In the Apostles' Creed we say that we believe in "the communion of saints."

By "the communion of saints" is meant the union of the faithful on earth, the blessed in heaven, and the souls in purgatory, with Christ as their Head.

The communion of saints is one big family. All who belong to the communion of saints in heaven, purgatory, and on earth love and help one another. We call it the communion of saints, because those in heaven are saints, the souls in purgatory will one day be saints, and the people on earth hope to be saints some day.

The saints in heaven help the souls in purgatory by praying for them. They help the members of the Church on earth by praying for them and by asking God for favors for them.

The souls in purgatory are suffering and being purified for their sins, but they will be able to help us by their prayers when they get to heaven. The people on earth can help the poor souls in purgatory by praying for them.

The saints in heaven who have their reward do not need the prayers of the people on earth. But we should honor them by our prayers and ask their help in all our needs. They are friends of God and our friends too.

The people on earth can help each other to become saints. How can we help do this? By praying for one another, by giving good example, and by performing the works of mercy.

The saints in heaven have had their sins forgiven. The souls in purgatory are suffering for theirs. The people on earth know that their sins can be forgiven, too, because every time they say the Apostles' Creed they say, "I believe in the forgiveness of sins."

By "the forgiveness of sins" in the Apostles' Creed is meant that God has given to the Church, through Jesus Christ, the power to forgive sins.

God's family is a very large one. If we are good members of His family on earth, we will be holy members of His family in heaven.

A SHORT PRAYER

O Virgin Mary, Mother of Jesus, make us saints.

FOR ME TO REVIEW

Catechism Lesson

1201. Q. What does the communion of saints mean?

A. The communion of saints means the union which exists between the members of the Church on earth with one another, and with the blessed in heaven, and with the suffering souls in purgatory.

734. Q. How do we know that our Lord, while on earth, had the power to forgive sins?

A. We know that our Lord, while on earth, had the power to forgive sins: 1) because He was always God, and 2) because He frequently did forgive sins and proved their forgiveness by miracles. Since He had the power Himself, He could give it to His Apostles.

85. Q. Through what means may we obtain the "forgiveness of sins"?

A. We may obtain the "forgiveness of sins" especially through the sacraments of Baptism and Penance and Reconciliation.

FOR ME TO REMEMBER

1. The saints in heaven, the souls in purgatory, and the people on earth form the communion of saints.
2. The members of the communion of saints all help one another.

FOR ME TO DO

1. Make a movie to show how the members of the Church on earth help one another.
2. Talk about how we can help Catholics in other countries. Then do it.

LESSON 56

What the Church Teaches About Life Everlasting—The Particular Judgment

Have you ever watched a leaf fall from a tree? Very quietly it leaves the living tree and flutters to the ground. What will happen to the leaf? It will dry up and crumble into dust, because it has been separated from the tree which gave it life.

Will the tree die because the leaf fell? No. The tree will continue to live.

Like the leaf, some day your body will be separated from your soul which gave it life. When this happens we say that you are dead.

Your body will be buried in the ground. There it will turn back to the dust from which it was made.

Your soul will never die. What will happen to it when it leaves your body?

As soon as you die Jesus, your Judge, will pass judgment on your soul. *The judgment which will be passed on each one of us immediately after death is called the particular judgment.*

If you die with sanctifying grace in your soul, it is because you have lived in friendship with God. When we die in perfect friendship with God, we will enter heaven. If we die having sin on our souls, even if we are still friends of God, we will go to purgatory. Purgatory purifies and cleanses our souls from venial sins. Have you ever broken something that did not belong to you? Perhaps you broke your mother's vase, and perhaps she forgives you. Does her forgiveness put the vase back together? No. The vase must be replaced, fixed, or paid for. In addition to cleansing the soul of venial sin, purgatory also purifies the soul of the effects of sin. After this purification, the soul ascends to heaven to be happy with God forever.

If your soul is without sanctifying grace when you die, it is because you have chosen to be an enemy of God. Those who choose a life of sin choose hell and suffer there after death for all eternity. Then some day you will be happy to hear Jesus say, "Come, you blessed of my Father, possess you the kingdom prepared for you from the foundation of the world" (Mt 25:34).

A SHORT PRAYER

Sweetest Jesus, be my Savior.

FOR ME TO REVIEW

Catechism Lesson

1372. Q. What is the judgment called which we have to undergo immediately after death?

A. The judgment we have to undergo immediately after death is called the particular judgment.

1378. Q. What are the rewards or punishments appointed for men's souls after the particular judgment?

A. The rewards or punishments appointed for men's souls after the particular judgment are heaven, purgatory, and hell.

FOR ME TO REMEMBER

1. Some day I must die. If I love God and keep His holy grace in my soul, I will enjoy friendship with God in heaven forever. If I do not love God and do not keep His holy grace in my soul, I will have chosen separation from God in hell forever.
2. The particular judgment takes place when the soul leaves the body.

FOR ME TO DO

1. Draw a picture of the story of the leaf found at the beginning of this lesson.
2. Make a picture book of good deeds you can do every day.
3. Each night say a "Hail Mary" asking our Blessed Lady and St. Joseph to be with you at the hour of death.
4. Discuss what you can do to help others to live in friendship with God in this life so that they might be happy with Him in heaven forever.

By the special favor of her Assumption, the glorified body of the Blessed Virgin Mary was taken into heaven.

LESSON 57

The General Judgment

On Easter Sunday, three days after Jesus died, He rose from the dead. The body of Jesus was joined to His soul, never again to be separated. We call this the Resurrection.

At the end of the world, your body will have a resurrection too. It will also rise from the dead.

By "the resurrection of the body" is meant that at the end of the world the bodies of all men will rise from the earth and be united again to their souls, nevermore to be separated.

There is one person who will have no resurrection of the body at the end of the world, our Blessed Mother. She received a special favor from God at the end of her life on earth. Do you know what it was? Mary's body did not turn back to dust. United to her soul, it was taken to heaven. We call this favor Mary's Assumption.

Why will your body rise from the dead? During your life your body had a part in your good or bad deeds. There is a reason, then, why your body should share in the reward or punishment that your soul will receive for those deeds. Your body and soul will be united again at the end of the world.

What will happen after your body rises from the dead? Jesus will come from heaven in His glory to pass judgment on all the people of the world.

The judgment which will be passed on all men immediately after the general resurrection is called the general judgment.

Jesus will tell the good people to stand at His right side. These will be the people who have chosen friendship with God and have lived in His grace. To them Jesus will say, "Come, you blessed of my Father, possess you the kingdom prepared for you from the foundation of the world" (Mt 25:34). These people, with body and soul united, will be taken to heaven forever.

To the wicked people standing at His left side, Jesus will say, "Depart from me, you cursed, into everlasting fire which was prepared for the devil and his angels" (Mt 25:41). These people, because they have chosen to live in sin and as an enemy of God, will be sent to hell forever.

Become a friend of Jesus. Friendship with God is truly the greatest happiness. If we live friendship with God now, by loving and serving Him, we will enjoy heaven for all eternity.

There is only one word of the Apostles' Creed that we have not studied this year. Do you know what it is? It is the tiny word "Amen." What does it mean? *By the word "Amen," with which we end the Apostles' Creed, is meant "So it is," or "So be it."*

A SHORT PRAYER

Lord Jesus Christ, allow me to enjoy friendship with You forever.

FOR ME TO REVIEW

Catechism Lesson

86. **Q. What do we mean by the "resurrection of the body"?**
A. By the "resurrection of the body" we mean that the bodies of the dead shall be restored to life, rise again on the last day, and be united to the souls from which they were separated by death.

1091. **Q. What do we mean by the Assumption of the Blessed Virgin, and why do we believe in it?**
A. By the Assumption of the Blessed Virgin we mean that her body was taken up into heaven after her dormition. We believe in it: 1) Because the Church cannot teach error, and yet from an early age the Church has celebrated the Feast of the Assumption; 2) because no one ever claimed to have a relic of our Blessed Mother's body, and surely the Apostles, who knew and loved her, would have secured some relic had her body remained upon earth.

1371. **Q. When will Christ judge us?**
A. Christ will judge us immediately after our death, and on the last day.

1374. **Q. What is the judgment called which all men have to undergo on the last day?**
A. The judgment which all men have to undergo on the last day is called the general judgment.

25. **Q. What does "Amen" mean?**
A. "Amen" means, "so be it" and expresses a desire that the petition may be granted.

FOR ME TO REMEMBER

1. Our bodies will rise from the dead at the end of the world. They will be united to our souls.
2. Our bodies and souls will share everlasting happiness in heaven or everlasting punishment in hell.
3. The Assumption means that the Blessed Virgin Mary was raised from the dead and taken body and soul into heaven.

FOR ME TO DO

1. Say the prayer to Mary from the Divine Praises.
2. Learn a prayer for a happy death.
3. Find a picture of the general judgment. Talk about it.

Write your answers on a separate sheet of paper

Part 1 Short Answer

1. On what day did Jesus send the Holy Spirit to the Apostles?
2. Why did Jesus start the Catholic Church?
3. Who is the present pope of the Catholic Church?
4. Who is the present bishop of our diocese?
5. Who belongs to the Catholic Church?
6. What are the marks of the Catholic Church?
7. What is meant by the communion of saints?
8. When will particular judgment take place?
9. When will general judgment take place?
10. What is the Assumption?

Part 2 Multiple Choice

Answer 1 to 5 on your own paper as you did before with A or B or C.

1. Jesus made the Apostles:
   A. popes.
   B. bishops.
   C. cardinals.
2. We became adopted children of God when we received the gift of:
   A. actual grace.
   B. sacramental grace.
   C. sanctifying grace.

3. The founder of the Catholic Church was:
   A. St. Peter.
   B. St. Joseph.
   C. Jesus Christ.

4. To help me say my prayer well I need:
   A. actual grace.
   B. sanctifying grace.
   C. sacramental grace.

5. Jesus started the Catholic Church:
   A. to bring everybody to heaven.
   B. to give us a place to pray.
   C. to give us a nice school.

Part 3 Completion

Write 1 to 10. After each number write the right answer from this list.

Holy Spirit	pope	apostolic
faith	one	purgatory
sacraments	sanctifying grace	sacrifice
Catholic	actual grace	

God's greatest gift to us is ______ (1).

The visible head of the Church is the ______ (2).

The Church is the congregation of all baptized persons who have the same true ______ (3), the same ______ (4), the same ______ (5), and are united under the pope.

The Church is ______ holy, catholic, and apostolic (6).

God's ______ will help me tell the truth (7).

The ______ makes the Church and its members holy (8).

The ______ Church is the true Church (9)

The members of the communion of saints are in heaven, on earth, or in ______ (10).

Part 4 Yes or No

On a separate sheet write 1 to 5 and answer each question with yes or no.

1. Did the Holy Spirit come down upon the Apostles on Pentecost?
2. Did Jesus make John his first pope?
3. Is the present pope the successor of St. Peter?
4. Is God's helping grace called sanctifying grace?
5. Can I get to heaven without God's helping grace?

CHAPTER 7
How We Love and Serve God

LESSON 58

The Law of Love

One day Jesus said to the people, "Not everyone who says to me, Lord, Lord, shall enter the kingdom of heaven; but he who does the will of my Father in heaven shall enter the kingdom of heaven."

By this Jesus meant that we must do more than believe God's truths if we expect to go to heaven. Do you know what else we must do? *Besides believing what God has revealed, we must keep His Law.*

The law that God expects us to keep is the law of love. This law is made up of two great commandments. These commandments contain the whole law of God.

The two great commandments that contain the whole law of God are: first, *Thou shalt love the Lord thy God with thy whole heart, and with thy whole soul, and with thy whole mind, and with thy whole strength; second, Thou shalt love thy neighbor as thyself.*

The love of God is the greatest commandment. If we truly love God, we will do nothing to offend Him. We will not commit sin, because sin is displeasing to Him. As we have learned, God is the Supreme Being as well as our loving Father. He has a right to command us to love Him. We are His creatures and should obey His commands.

Our Lord said: "Thou shalt love thy neighbor as thyself." We should love our neighbor too, because he also is a child of God and made to God's image. God loves him so much that He died to redeem him. Our neighbor is to live forever in heaven with God, so we should love him for God's sake.

We are made to God's image also; therefore we must love God's image in ourselves. We are redeemed by the blood of Christ, so we must remember that we are very precious in God's sight. By the merits of Jesus Christ we are made children of God, heirs of heaven, and temples of the Holy Spirit; therefore, we should love ourselves to show love for God. We are to live forever in heaven with God; therefore we should love ourselves enough to keep away from sin and to practice virtue.

What must we do to love God, our neighbor, and ourselves? *To love God, our neighbor, and ourselves we must keep the commandments of God and of the Church.*

How were these commandments given to us? Moses spent forty days on Mount Sinai speaking to God. Then God gave him two stone tablets on which were written the Ten Commandments. The first three commandments tell about our duties to God. The other seven commandments point out our duties toward our neighbor. *The commandments of God are these ten:*

1. **I am the Lord thy God; thou shalt not have strange gods before Me.**
2. **Thou shalt not take the name of the Lord thy God in vain.**
3. **Remember thou keep holy the Lord's day.**
4. **Honor thy father and thy mother.**
5. **Thou shalt not kill.**
6. **Thou shalt not commit adultery.**
7. **Thou shalt not steal.**
8. **Thou shalt not bear false witness against thy neighbor.**
9. **Thou shalt not covet thy neighbor's wife.**
10. **Thou shalt not covet thy neighbor's goods.**

By keeping God's commandments we prove our love for Him.

A SHORT PRAYER

Sweet Heart of Jesus, be my love.

FOR ME TO REVIEW

Catechism Lesson

84. **Q. Besides believing what God has revealed, what else must we do to be saved?**

    A. Besides believing what God has revealed, we must keep His law.

85. **Q. Which are the two great commandments that contain the whole law of God?**

    A. The two great commandments that contain the whole law of God are: *first,* Thou shalt love the Lord thy God with thy whole heart, and with thy whole soul, and with thy whole mind, and with thy whole strength; Z Thou shalt love thy neighbor as thyself.

86. **Q. What must we do to love God, our neighbor, and ourselves?**

    A. To love God, our neighbor, and ourselves we must keep the commandments of God and of the Church.

87. **Q. Which are the commandments of God?**

    A. The commandments of God are these ten:

    1. I am the Lord thy God; thou shalt not have strange gods before Me.
    2. Thou shalt not take the name of the Lord thy God in vain.
    3. Remember thou keep holy the Lord's day.
    4. Honor thy father and thy mother.
    5. Thou shalt not kill.
    6. Thou shalt not commit adultery.

7. Thou shalt not steal.
8. Thou shalt not bear false witness against thy neighbor.
9. Thou shalt not covet thy neighbor's wife.
10. Thou shalt not covet thy neighbor's goods.

FOR ME TO REMEMBER

1. The Law of God is the law of love.
2. We must love God and our neighbor as ourselves.
3. We prove our love for God by obedience to His commandments.

FOR ME TO DO

1. Make a picture of the stone tablets on which the Ten Commandments were written.
2. Write the Ten Commandments, and memorize them.
3. Tell the story of God giving the Ten Commandments, or dramatize it.

LESSON 59

The First Commandment and How We Keep It

The first commandment of God is: I am the Lord thy God; thou shalt not have strange gods before Me.

God gave us the Ten Commandments because He wanted all people to know that He is the Supreme Being. He wanted everyone to love Him above all things.

Each of God's Ten Commandments tells us something that we must do to get to heaven. *By the first commandment we are commanded to offer to God alone the supreme worship that is due Him.*

God is the Supreme Being who made the whole world. He is all-good, all-wise, and all-powerful. God must have more honor and love and praise than anyone else in the world. God commands us, to worship Him and Him alone.

Today there are people in the world who do not adore Him as the Supreme Being. They adore false gods. Some people in India worship a sacred cow. Other people in Japan worship Buddha, and the pagan Indians worship god in nature.

Some of our own American people worship money, their cars, their sports and clothes. They love these things more than they love God. Therefore we could call these things false gods. It is wrong

for Catholics to worship false gods because we know that God is the Supreme Being, our Creator and Father. God commands that everyone worship Him, and love Him above all things.

How do we worship God? *We worship God by acts of faith, hope, and charity, and by adoring Him and praying to Him.*

We worship God by faith when we believe all His truths. We worship God by hope when we trust that He will forgive us our sins and give us the help we need to get to heaven. We worship God by charity when we love Him more than anything else in the world.

We also worship God by adoring Him. Do you know what that means? We adore God by telling Him by our words and actions that He is the Giver of all good things. We adore God by telling Him that we want to live with Him in heaven when we die. We adore God by telling Him that we can do nothing without His help.

We worship God by praying to Him. You have been praying to God for many years, but do you know what prayer really is? Prayer is raising our minds and hearts to God. Prayer is talking to God. Prayer is also thinking of God. Each time we turn our thoughts to God or whisper loving words to Him, we are praying.

What kind of prayers can we say? We can say the prayers we know by heart. We can read prayers from our prayer books, or we can talk to God in our own words. Our prayers can be as long or short as we want them to be. What prayer is the best prayer of all?

When we pray we must try to keep our mind on what we are saying. We must mean the words that we say. We must pray from our hearts and not with our lips only. If we pray like this, we are lifting our hearts and minds to God.

Our bodies help us to pray well, too. When we kneel down to pray, we show God that we believe He is the Lord and the Maker of us all. When we fold our hands we show God that we are His servants.

Must we pray only to God? No. God also wants us to pray to His Blessed Mother, His angels and His friends, the saints. But this prayer is not the same as the worship we give to God when we pray to Him. Can you name some saints to whom we should pray?

God wants us to think of Him and talk to Him every day. That is why we say morning and night prayers, and prayers before and after meals. God wants us to ask Him for His help whenever we are in danger. God wants us to think of Him as often as we can.

Today there are many people who do not know the true God. They worship false gods. Our missionary priests and sisters are trying to tell all pagans about the one true God. Their work is not easy. The priests and sisters need our prayers to help them in their work.

A SHORT PRAYER

O Most Holy Trinity I adore Thee who art dwelling by Thy grace within my soul.

FOR ME TO REVIEW

Catechism Lesson

88. **Q. What is the first commandment of God?**

    A. The first commandment of God is: I am the Lord thy God; thou shalt not have strange gods before Me.

89. **Q. What are we commanded by the first commandment?**

    A. By the first commandment we are commanded to offer to God alone the supreme worship that is due Him.

90. **Q. How do we worship God?**

    A. We worship God by acts of faith, hope, and charity, and by adoring Him and praying to Him.

FOR ME TO REMEMBER

1. The first commandment tells us to worship God alone.
2. We worship God by acts of faith, hope, and charity and by adoring Him and praying to Him.
3. When we pray we lift up our minds and hearts to God.

FOR ME TO DO

1. Make up your own little acts of faith, hope, and charity. Say them in church.
2. Talk about little acts that show our faith, hope, and love. Then do some of them.

LESSON 60

The First Commandment and How We Break It

God gave us the Ten Commandments to help us get to heaven. Every time we obey one of God's laws we do as God wants us to do. Every time we break one of God's laws we commit a sin.

Let us see how we might break the first commandment.

We know that God wants us to pray. If we never say our morning and night prayers, or we do not try to pray well, we can commit a sin against the first commandment.

We also break the first commandment if we sin against the virtues of faith, hope, or charity.

How does a Catholic sin against faith? *A Catholic sins against faith by not believing what God has revealed.* We must believe everything God teaches us through the Catholic Church. If we do not believe God's truths we commit a sin against faith. We must also worship God by assisting at Holy Mass and devotions in the Catholic Church, which is the true Church of God.

What are the sins against hope? *The sins against hope are presumption and despair.*

We commit the sin of presumption if we think that we can get to heaven without God's help. We also commit the sin of presumption if we think we can go to heaven without living a good life. If a man would say, "I will continue to commit as many sins as I please during my life and when I am dying I will tell God I am sorry for these sins," that man would be guilty of the sin of presumption.

A man commits the sin of despair if he denies that God is good and merciful and is willing to forgive all of his sins. This man refuses to believe that God is all-merciful and can forgive all sins if we tell Him we are sorry for them.

There are many sins against the virtue of charity, but *the chief sins against charity are hatred of God and of our neighbor, envy, sloth, and scandal.*

Certainly, to hate God and our neighbor is very wrong. A person who hates God and his neighbor will not keep the commandments. Neither will a person who is slothful or lazy. He will not pray. He will not always go to Mass on Sunday. He will not try to be a good Catholic.

A person who is not a good Catholic gives scandal to others. His sins may cause others to commit the same sins. A Catholic mother and father who do not go to Mass on Sunday give scandal to their children.

If we hate our neighbor, we will also be jealous of him. We will not be happy unless we have everything that he has. We will be guilty of the sin of envy.

If you love God and your neighbor, you will always try to keep the first commandment of God. God will be pleased, and you will be happy.

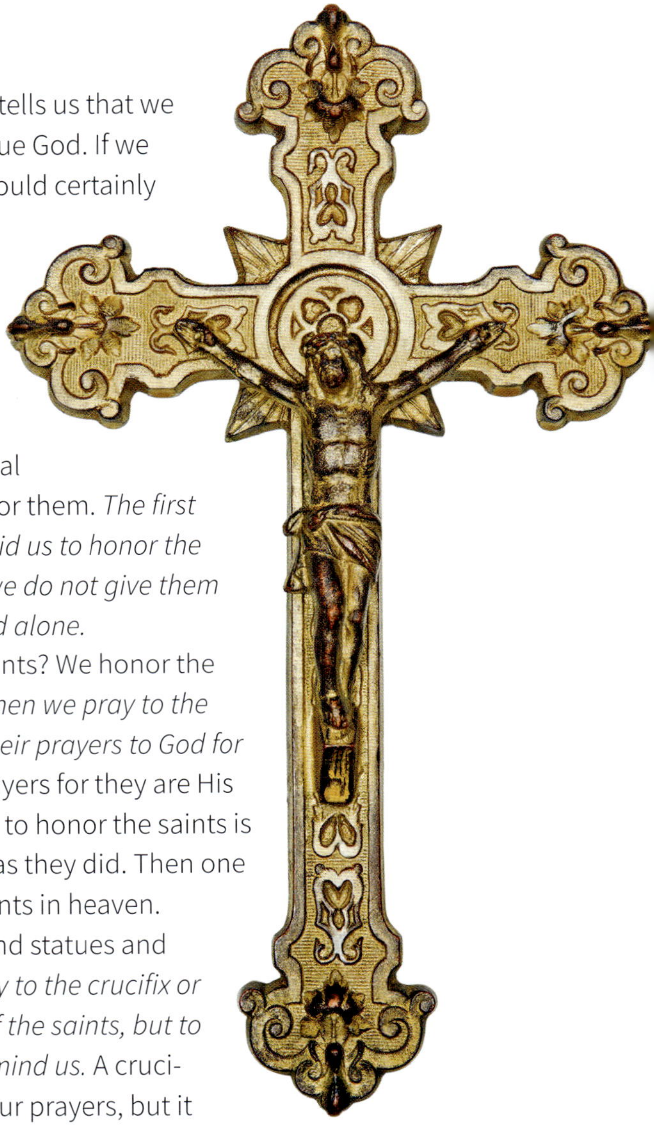

The first commandment tells us that we must worship only the one true God. If we worshiped false gods, that would certainly be a great sin. God alone is the Supreme Being who is worshiped in the Catholic Church.

Do we worship the saints? No, we honor them, because they are God's special friends. God wants us to honor them. *The first commandment does not forbid us to honor the saints in heaven, as long as we do not give them the honor that belongs to God alone.*

How do we honor the saints? We honor the saints by praying to them. *When we pray to the saints we ask them to offer their prayers to God for us.* God will listen to their prayers for they are His special friends. The best way to honor the saints is to try to love and serve God as they did. Then one day we, too, will be God's saints in heaven.

Do we pray to pictures and statues and crucifixes? No, *we do not pray to the crucifix or to the images of Christ and of the saints, but to the persons of whom they remind us.* A crucifix or a picture cannot hear our prayers, but it reminds us of the person to whom we are praying, and helps us to pray better.

A SHORT PRAYER

Vouchsafe, O Lord, this day to keep us without sin.

Faith in God's love encompasses the call and the obligation to respond with sincere love to divine charity. The first commandment enjoins us to love God above everything and all creatures for him and because of him.

—Catechism of the Catholic Church, 2093

FOR ME TO REVIEW

Catechism Lesson

91. **Q. How does a Catholic sin against faith?**
    A. A Catholic sins against faith by not believing what God has revealed.

92. **Q. What are the sins against hope?**
    A. The sins against hope are presumption and despair.

93. **Q. What are the chief sins against charity?**
    A. The chief sins against charity are hatred of God and of our neighbor, envy, sloth, and scandal.

94. **Q. Does the first commandment forbid us to honor the saints in heaven?**
A. The first commandment does not forbid us to honor the saints in heaven, as long as we do not give them the honor that belongs to God alone.

95. **Q. When we pray to the saints what do we ask them to do?**
A. When we pray to the saints we ask them to offer their prayers to God for us.

96. **Q. Do we pray to the crucifix or to the images of Christ and of the saints?**
A. We do not pray to the crucifix or to the images of Christ and of the saints, but to the persons of whom they remind us.

FOR ME TO REMEMBER

1. We can sin against the first commandment in these ways:
   a) By neglecting to say our daily prayers for a long time.
   b) By praying carelessly.
   c) By not believing God's truths.
   d) By committing the sins of presumption and despair.
   e) By hating God and our neighbor.
   f) By committing the sins of sloth, envy, and scandal.

FOR ME TO DO

1. Examine your conscience to see how well you keep God's first commandment.
2. Tell God you are sorry for any sins committed today.
3. Find out all you can about your patron saint.

LESSON 61

The Second Commandment and How We Keep It

The second commandment of God is: Thou shalt not take the name of the Lord Thy God in vain.

We keep the second commandment by speaking with love and respect about God, the saints, and holy things.

If we use God's name in a prayer, or if we speak about God in a nice way, we are using His name with reverence.

The saints are holy people too. God wants us to speak with reverence about them. Do you know the names of some of the saints?

God also wants us to speak with reverence about holy things. Can you name some of them?

> *"To holy people the very name of Jesus is a name to feed upon, a name to transport. His name can raise the dead and transfigure and beautify the living."*
>
> *—Saint John Henry Newman*

By the second commandment we are commanded always to speak with reverence of God, of the saints, and of holy things.

Long ago, people felt that God's name was so holy that they seldom ever said it.

Today we say the name of God many times in our prayers. We often call upon the name of God before we start or finish our work, when we are in trouble, when we are sick, and when we are in danger.

The name of Jesus is the most powerful of all names. Many people use the name of Jesus to send the devil away when he tempts them. They use the name of Jesus many times during the day in many little prayers.

We show reverence and love for the name of Jesus by bowing our heads every time we speak it or hear it spoken. We should especially say the name of Jesus at the hour of our death. Remember it means Savior. By the name of Jesus the Apostles and saints worked many miracles as St. Peter did when he said to the lame man, "In the name of Jesus Christ, arise and walk." Holy Scripture says, "There is no other name under heaven given to man, by which we must be saved."

A SHORT PRAYER

Blessed be the name of the Lord.

FOR ME TO REVIEW

Catechism Lesson

97. Q. What is the second commandment of God?

A. The second commandment of God is: Thou shalt not take the name of the Lord thy God in vain.

98. **Q. What are we commanded by the second commandment?**

A. By the second commandment we are commanded always to speak with reverence of God, of the saints, and of holy things.

FOR ME TO REMEMBER

1. The second commandment tells us to use the holy name of God with reverence.
2. We must speak with reverence of holy people, holy places, and holy things.
3. The name of Jesus is very powerful.

FOR ME TO DO

1. Try to get the good habit of saying the holy name of Jesus many times during the day.
2. Bow your head every time you say the holy name of Jesus or hear it spoken.
3. Say the Divine Praises with attention and devotion.
4. Find pictures of holy people and holy things. Paste them in a book.

LESSON 62

The Second Commandment and How We Break It

Today many people use God's holy name and the name of Jesus without reverence. They use these holy names when they are angry. Sometimes they use these holy names when they are making fun. They are using God's holy name in vain and committing sin. *By taking God's name in vain is meant that the name of God or the holy name of Jesus Christ is used without reverence.*

What can we do if we hear someone using God's holy name the wrong way? We can whisper a little prayer to make up for their sin. This would be a very good prayer to say: "Blessed be the name of Jesus." Can we do anything else? Yes, we can tell people to use God's name the right way.

We can also sin against the second commandment by making fun of God or saying mean things about Him, about the saints, and about holy things.

Cursing is another sin against the second commandment. Do you know what cursing is? *Cursing is the calling down of some evil on a person, place, or thing.* If we ask God to make some evil or terrible thing happen to someone, we would be cursing him. We must wish only good things on persons, places, and things, even if we dislike them.

When Jesus comes to you in Holy Communion your tongue is His first resting place. It is like the chalice at Mass. Ask Jesus to help you use your tongue to praise Him. Also ask our Blessed Mother to help you use God's holy name with love and reverence at all times.

A SHORT PRAYER

Sacred Heart of Jesus, convert all poor blasphemers.

FOR ME TO REVIEW

Catechism Lesson

99. **Q. What is meant by taking God's name in vain?**
    A. By taking God's name in vain is meant that the name of God or the holy name of Jesus Christ is used without reverence.

Q. 100. What is cursing?
    A. Cursing is the calling down of some evil on a person, place, or thing.

FOR ME TO REMEMBER

1. We break the second commandment:
   a) By using God's holy name when we are angry.
   b) By using God's holy name when we are making fun.
   c) By saying mean things about God, holy people, holy places, or holy things.
   d) By making fun of holy people, holy places, or holy things.
   e) By cursing.

FOR ME TO DO

1. Pray every day for those who use God's name in the wrong way.
2. Recite the Divine Praises to make up for the sins against the second commandment.
3. Say the holy name with reverence when someone uses it the wrong way.

LESSON 63

The Third Commandment and How We Keep It

The third commandment of God is: Remember thou keep holy the Lord's day.

Sunday is the Lord's day. It is holy. It is the day on which we must rest from our work and give God special honor by assisting devoutly at Holy Mass. God commanded us to give this day to Him when He said, "Six days may you labor and do all your work, but the seventh day is the Sabbath of the Lord your God." *By the third commandment we are commanded to worship God in a special manner on Sunday, the Lord's day.*

How does the Church command us to worship God on Sunday? *The Church commands us to worship God on Sunday by participating in the Holy Sacrifice of the Mass.*

We know that the best way in which God can be honored is by the Holy Sacrifice of the Mass. That is why the Church commands that all Catholics must honor God every Sunday by participating in Holy Mass.

Besides participating in Holy Mass on Sunday, is there anything else we can do to keep the Lord's day holy? We can attend Benediction of the Blessed Sacrament. We can read holy books. We can say extra prayers. We can also visit our relatives, friends, the poor, and the sick. By doing these things we can sanctify the Lord's day and bring down God's blessing upon us and upon our work for the coming week.

A SHORT PRAYER

Immaculate Queen of Peace, pray for us.

FOR ME TO REVIEW

Catechism Lesson

101. Q. What is the third commandment of God?

A. The third commandment of God is: Remember thou keep holy the Lord's day.

102. Q. What are we commanded by the third commandment?

A. By the third commandment we are commanded to worship God in a special manner on Sunday, the Lord's day.

103. Q. How does the Church command us to worship God on Sunday?

A. The Church commands us to worship God on Sunday by participating in the Holy Sacrifice of the Mass.

FOR ME TO REMEMBER

1. Sunday is the Lord's day.
2. We must participate in the Holy Mass every Sunday.
3. Sunday is a day of rest and a day to do good works.

FOR ME TO DO

1. Make a list of good works that you can do on Sunday.
2. Draw a picture of a child keeping Sunday holy.
3. Talk about how we should keep Sunday holy.

LESSON 64

The Third Commandment and How We Break It

By the third commandment we are commanded to worship God in a special way on Sunday, the Lord's day. Catholics worship God in this special way by participating in Mass.

To miss Mass on Sunday without a good reason is a grave sin. If we miss Mass on Sunday, we do not give God the honor that is His due.

To come late for Mass on Sunday is a venial sin unless we have a good reason for being late. If for no good reason we are not in church when the Offertory begins or if we leave before the priest received Holy Communion we miss Mass and commit a grave sin.

If Sunday is a day of rest, may we do any work on that day? *By the third commandment of God all unnecessary work on Sunday is forbidden.*

Some work on Sunday is necessary and some is not. If we do hard work on Sunday and it is not necessary that we do it on that day, we commit a sin. God will not bless the unnecessary work that we do on Sunday. Can you think of some kinds of work that must be done on Sunday?

We know that if we keep Sunday holy, God will bless us and keep us holy.

A SHORT PRAYER

Draw us after thee, holy Mother.

FOR ME TO REVIEW

Catechism Lesson

104. Q. What is forbidden by the third commandment of God?

A. By the third commandment of God all unnecessary work on Sunday is forbidden.

FOR ME TO REMEMBER

1. We break the third commandment:
   a) By missing Mass on Sunday without a good reason.
   b) By being late for Mass on Sunday without a good reason.
   c) By doing unnecessary work on Sunday.

FOR ME TO DO

1. Assist at Mass devoutly.
2. Use your prayer book during Mass.
3. Try to kneel up straight during Mass.

4. Be on time for Mass every Sunday.
5. Write a three sentence story thanking God for the Holy Sacrifice of the Mass.
6. Talk about how you can help your family and your neighbors keep the Lord's day holy.

LESSON 65

The Last Seven Commandments of God

This year we study the first three commandments of God to help us know, love, and serve God better. In a later grade we will learn how to love our neighbor as ourselves for the love of God by keeping the commandments from the fourth to the tenth. Now we will take just a short look at them.

The fourth commandment tells us to love, respect, and obey our parents and all who take care of us.

The fifth commandment tells us to be kind to others. It also tells us to take care of the life of our bodies and our souls and of the bodies and souls of our neighbors.

The sixth commandment tells us to be pure. It also tells us to be modest in our behavior.

The seventh commandment tells us to be honest and not to steal, cheat, or damage the property of others.

The eighth commandment tells us to tell the truth in all things and to say only good things about our neighbor.

The ninth commandment tells us to keep our thoughts and desires pure and modest.

The tenth commandment tells us not to wish to take or to keep unjustly what belongs to others. It also tells us not to envy others their success.

God loves you. He will never stop loving you. Do you want to love God forever? If you do, keep the commandments. Then you will be sure to love God forever.

A SHORT PRAYER

Jesus, meek and humble of heart, make my heart like unto Thine.

FOR ME TO REVIEW

Questions

1. Tell which children are trying to offer worship to God.
   a) Mabel says her night prayers only when she is not tired.
   b) Harry stays home from church on Sunday when he wants to sleep in.
   c) Joan goes to Mass every morning.
   d) Robert whispers a little prayer to Jesus every time he looks at a crucifix.
   e) Frank folds his hands and thinks of God whenever he prays.
2. Which children are showing respect for the name of God?
   a) Kate laughs when she hears her playmate use God's name in anger.
   b) Carl bows his head whenever he hears someone say the holy name of Jesus.
   c) Bill is trying to break the bad habit of using God's name in vain.
   d) Donald uses God's name in the wrong way because he thinks it makes him sound "grown-up."
   e) Betty whispers the name of Jesus and Mary many times every day.
   f) John says the holy name of Jesus whenever the devil tempts him to sin.

3. Which phrases make you think of the first commandment? the second? the third?
   a) Hearing Mass on Sunday.
   b) Bowing your head when you hear the name of Jesus.
   c) Visiting the sick.
   d) Saying your morning and night prayers every day.
   e) Wishing good to everyone.
   f) Believing everything that the Church teaches.
   g) Reading a holy book.
   h) Praying before a statue of the Blessed Mother in your bedroom.
   i) Telling other children to keep God's name holy.

FOR ME TO REMEMBER

1. The last seven commandments of God tell us how to love our neighbor as ourselves.

FOR ME TO DO

1. Obey promptly all that your parents tell or ask you to do.
2. Practice little acts of kindness toward others every day.
3. Say three Hail Marys to our Lady every night for the virtue of purity.
4. Play fair today and be honest in all your dealings with others.
5. Tell the truth in order not to offend God rather than avoid punishment.
6. Make a movie to show how we love our neighbor.

Write your answers on a separate sheet of paper

Part 1 Short Answer

1. How do we love and serve God?
2. Name the Ten Commandments.
3. Who gave us the Ten Commandments?
4. What two commandments contain the whole law of God?
5. How must we love our neighbor?
6. What does the first commandment tell us to do?
7. How do we worship God?
8. Who are the saints?
9. How do we honor the saints?
10. What is prayer?
11. How must we pray?
12. Can we be saved if we never pray?
13. What does the second commandment tell us to do?
14. Why must we keep God's name holy?
15. How do we break the second commandment?
16. What does the third commandment tell us to do?
17. How do we keep Sunday holy?

Part 2 Yes or No

On a separate paper write 1 to 5 and answer each question with yes or no.

1. Some day will everyone in the world know that there is only one God?
2. Do I commit an original sin if I miss Mass on Sunday through my own fault?
3. Is the Mass the highest form of worship?
4. Does God want us to honor the saints?
5. Do we pray to statues?

Part 3 Matching

Write 1 to 5 on another paper. After each number write the letter which is in front of the correct answer.

1. Second commandment	A. The law that tells us to worship God.
2. First commandment	B. The Lord's day.
3. Sunday	C. Talking to God.
4. Prayer	D. The law that tells us to keep God's name holy.

Part 4 Multiple Choice

Write 1 to 5 on another paper. After each number write the letter A or B or C as you did before.

1. We love God when we:
   A. do as we please.
   B. obey His commandments.
   C. miss Mass on Sunday.
2. We pray to God because:
   A. He needs our prayers.
   B. God does not care what we do.
   C. we need His help.
3. The first three commandments tell us how:
   A. to love God.
   B. to love our neighbor.
   C. to love ourselves.
4. When we take God's name in vain we sin against:
   A. the first commandment.
   B. the second commandment.
   C. the third commandment.
5. We should participate in Mass on Sunday because:
   A. we have new clothes.
   B. God commanded us to keep His day holy.
   C. we can visit with our friends.

Part 5 Completion

Complete the sentences on another sheet of paper.

1. The first commandment tells us to ______.
2. The second commandment forbids ______.
3. The most important thing that we must do on Sunday is ______.

Prayers

The Sign of the Cross

In the name of the Father, and of the Son, and of the Holy Spirit. Amen.

The Lord's Prayer

Our Father who art in heaven, hallowed be Thy name; Thy kingdom come; Thy will be done on earth as it is in heaven. Give us this day our daily bread; and forgive us our trespasses as we forgive those who trespass against us; and lead us not into temptation, but deliver us from evil. Amen.

The Hail Mary

Hail Mary, full of grace, the Lord is with thee; blessed art thou among women, and blessed is the fruit of thy womb, Jesus. Holy Mary, Mother of God, pray for us sinners, now and at the hour of our death. Amen.

Glory Be to the Father

Glory be to the Father, and to the Son, and to the Holy Spirit. As it was in the beginning, is now, and ever shall be, world without end. Amen.

The Apostles' Creed

I believe in God, the Father Almighty, Creator of heaven and earth; and in Jesus Christ, His only Son, Our Lord; who was conceived by the Holy Spirit, born of the Virgin Mary, suffered under Pontius Pilate, was crucified, died, and was buried. He descended into hell; the third day He arose again from the dead; He ascended into heaven, and sits at the right hand of God, the Father Almighty; from thence He shall come to judge the living and the dead. I believe in the Holy Spirit, the Holy Catholic Church, the communion of saints, the forgiveness of sins, the resurrection of the body, and life everlasting. Amen.

An Act of Faith

O my God, I firmly believe that Thou art one God in three Divine Persons, Father, Son, and Holy Spirit; I believe that Thy Divine Son became man, and died for our sins, and that He will come to judge the living and the dead. I believe these and all the truths which the Holy Catholic Church teaches, because Thou hast revealed them, who canst neither deceive nor be deceived.

An Act of Hope

O my God, relying on Thy almighty power and infinite mercy and promises, I hope to obtain pardon of my sins, the help of Thy grace, and life everlasting, through the merits of Jesus Christ, my Lord and Redeemer.

An Act of Love

O my God, I love Thee above all things, with my whole heart and soul, because Thou art all-good and worthy of all love. I love my neighbor as myself for the love of Thee. I forgive all who have injured me, and ask pardon of all whom I have injured.

An Act of Contrition

O my God, I am heartily sorry for having offended Thee, and I detest all my sins, because of Thy just punishments, but most of all because they offend Thee, my God, who art all-good and deserving of all my love. I firmly resolve, with the help of Thy grace, to sin no more and to avoid the near occasions of sin.

Morning Offering

O Jesus, through the Immaculate Heart of Mary, I offer Thee my prayers, works, joys and sufferings of this day for all the intentions of Thy Sacred Heart, in union with the Holy Sacrifice of the Mass throughout the world, in reparation for my sins, for the intentions of all our relatives and friends, and in particular for the intentions of the Hold Father. Amen.

The Angelus

V. The angel of the Lord declared unto Mary.
R. And she conceived of the Holy Spirit.

Hail Mary, full of grace! the Lord is with thee; blessed art thou among women, and blessed is the fruit of thy womb, Jesus. Holy Mary, Mother of God, pray for us sinners, now and at the hour of our death. Amen.

V. Behold the handmaid of the Lord.
R. Be it done unto me according to thy word.

Hail Mary, etc.

V. And the Word was made flesh.
R. And dwelt among us.

Hail Mary, etc.

V. Pray for us, O holy Mother of God.
R. That we may be made worthy of the promises of Christ.

Let Us Pray
Pour forth, we beseech Thee, O Lord, Thy grace into our hearts, that we to whom the Incarnation of Christ, Thy Son, was made known by the message of an angel, may by His passion and cross be brought to the glory of His resurrection, through the same Christ Our Lord. Amen.

Regina Coeli

(Said during Eastertide, instead of the Angelus)

Queen of heaven, rejoice, Alleluia.
For He whom thou didst deserve to bear, Alleluia.
Hath risen as He said, Alleluia.
Pray for us to God, Alleluia.
V. Rejoice and be glad, O Virgin Mary! Alleluia.
R. Because Our Lord is truly risen, Alleluia.

Let Us Pray
O God, who by the resurrection of Thy Son, Our Lord Jesus Christ, have vouchsafed to make glad the whole world, grant, we beseech Thee, that, through the intercession of the Virgin Mary, His Mother, we may attain the joys of eternal life. Through the same Christ Our Lord. Amen.

Hail, Holy Queen

Hail, Holy Queen, Mother of Mercy; hail, our life, our sweetness, and our hope! To thee do we cry, poor banished children of Eve; to thee we do send up our sighs, mourning and weeping in this vale of tears. Turn, then, most gracious advocate, thine eyes of mercy toward us; and after this our exile, show unto us the blessed fruit of thy womb, Jesus. O clement, O loving, O sweet Virgin Mary!

A Prayer to St. Michael

St. Michael, the Archangel, defend us in battle, be our defense against the wickedness and snares of the devil. May God rebuke him, we humbly pray; and do thou, O Prince of the heavenly host, by the power of God, thrust into hell Satan and the other evil spirits who prowl about the world for the ruin of souls. Amen.

The Blessing Before Meals

Bless us, O Lord, and these Thy gifts, which we are about to receive from Thy bounty, through Christ Our Lord. Amen.

Grace After Meals

We give Thee thanks for all Thy benefits, O Almighty God, who livest and reignest forever; and may the souls of the faithful departed, through the mercy of God, rest in peace. Amen.

The Mysteries of the Rosary

The Five Joyful Mysteries

1. The Annunciation
2. The Visitation
3. The Birth of Our Lord
4. The Presentation of Our Lord in the Temple
5. The Finding of Our Lord in the Temple

The Five Luminous Mysteries

1. The Baptism of Our Lord in the Jordan
2. The Wedding Feast at Cana
3. Our Lord's Proclamation of the Kingdom of God
4. The Transfiguration of Our Lord
5. The Institution of the Eucharist

The Five Sorrowful Mysteries

1. The Agony of Our Lord in the Garden
2. The Scourging at the Pillar
3. The Crowning With Thorns
4. The Carrying of the Cross
5. The Crucifixion and Death of Our Lord

The Five Glorious Mysteries

1. The Resurrection of Our Lord
2. The Ascension of Our Lord into Heaven
3. The Descent of the Holy Spirit Upon the Apostles
4. The Assumption of Our Blessed Mother into Heaven
5. The Coronation of Our Blessed Mother in Heaven

The Immaculate Conception with the Fifteen Mysteries of the Rosary

Answer Key

Chapter 1

Lesson 2

Questions

1. God is the Supreme Being who made all things.
2. He is above all creatures, no one is as great as He.
3. He made us because He is good. He made us to show His goodness.
4. No, God does not need us. He did it out of love.
5. It will be forever and more perfect than on earth.
6. Because Jesus founded it and it teaches what He taught.
7. We are taught by the Catholic Church.
8. Because it contains the chief truths taught by Jesus Christ.
9. We are all made for heaven.
10. You can try to let her know about some of the truths found in the Catholic Church, specifically in the Apostles' Creed.
11. By sharing the truths of the Catholic Church.

Lesson 5

Questions

1. Yes, it will allow him to make a good confession.
2. He must be sorry for his sins, strive to sin no more, and avoid the near occasion of sin.
3. No, mortal sin is dangerous for the soul because it removes sanctifying grace and separates you from God, confession is the only sure way to restore sanctifying grace to someone who has committed mortal sin.

To Prove My Mastery, Lessons 1–8

Part 1. Short Answer

1. God made all things.
2. Out of love, so we could know Him.

3. Stay in a state of sanctifying grace.
4. Learn about God through the Church and receive the Holy Eucharist.
5. Learning about God and being close to Him is our purpose on earth until the time we can know him better.
6. To follow His commandments.
7. The Church
8. Though the Apostles' Creed, Tradition and Scripture.
9. The Apostles' Creed
10. Penance and Reconciliation is a sacrament in which the sins committed after Baptism are forgiven.
11. Jesus gave the sacrament of Penance and Reconciliation.
12. 1. I must think of my sins. 2. I must be sorry for my sins. 3. I must make up my mind not to sin again. 4. I must tell my sins to the priest. 5. I must do my penance.
13. Being sorry for my sins.
14. Because it is a sin to lie in confession.
15. To make up some of the punishment for my sins.
16. When we receive the body and blood of Jesus.
17. Jesus gave us the sacrament at the Last Supper so that He can be near us and so that we can receive grace.
18. 1. My soul must be free from mortal sin. 2. I must fast one hour before Mass. 3. I must pray.
19. I must talk to Jesus through prayer.
20. He gives your soul grace.
21. I can pray and receive the sacraments often.

Part 2: Yes or No

1. Yes
2. No
3. Yes
4. Yes
5. Yes

6. No
7. Yes
8. Yes
9. Yes

Part 3: Completion

1. goodness
2. Holy Eucharist
3. Penance and Reconciliation
4. grace
5. Apostles' Creed
6. forgive
7. Catholic Church
8. five
9. Confession
10. happiness

Part 4: Match the letter and numbers

1. C
2. A
3. D
4. B
5. E

Part 5: Multiple Choice

1. B
2. C
3. C
4. A
5. B

Chapter 2

Lesson 19

Questions

1. God gave us the sacraments, God gave us His Church, God gives us guardian angels, God watches over us at all times.
2. The sign of the cross, the Apostles' Creed, and the Nicene Creed.
3. All three persons of the Trinity are God and are equally God, so there is no greatest person of the Trinity.
4. He can use a shamrock and explain that there are three leaves but they are still only one shamrock, like the shamrock God is three persons, God the Father, the Son and the Holy Spirit, but one God. However, all analogies fall short in trying to explain the Blessed Trinity.
5. All sins show that we do not love God as He should be loved. Also we are punished for venial sins.
6. a, d, e
7. I should do an act of contrition then go to confession as soon as possible by either going when there is confession scheduled or schedule confession with a priest myself. You want to receive confession because a mortal sin separates you from God and sanctifying grace which you need to go to heaven.
8. My praying and receiving the sacraments and working hard to build good habits.

To Prove My Mastery, Lessons 9–19

Part 1. Short Answer

1. God is infinitely perfect.
2. God's perfection is eternal and complete.
3. God is perfectly good, just, loving, and all-knowing.
4. Eternal
5. Because He is the creator, no one created Him.
6. God is all-knowing

7. God is everywhere
8. Because He loves us so much.
9. God is all powerful.
10. Though His creation, through His Son and His miracles.
11. Yes, there is only one God.
12. There are three persons in God.
13. God the Father, God the Son, and God the Holy Spirit
14. God the Son
15. God the Father
16. God the Holy Spirit
17. God the Holy Spirit
18. God the Father
19. God the Son
20. Because he created heaven and earth from nothing.
21. Because God made us.
22. The angels and men.
23. Because they were made to know and share in God's happiness.
24. Yes, God created the angels before creating the world.
25. Angels were originally made than men because they received a greater power of understanding. By taking on human nature, Jesus elevated men above angels.
26. They help us by praying for us, by acting as messengers from God to us, and by serving as guardian angels.
27. They live in hell and try to make us sin so we join them in hell.
28. They received bodies, minds, immortal souls, free wills, and sanctifying grace.
29. Sanctifying grace
30. He gave them a commandment not to eat of the fruit of a certain tree in the garden of paradise.
31. Adam and Eve lost sanctifying grace and the right to heaven and were driven from the Garden of Eden.

32. Original sin
33. We come into the world without grace, and we suffer from labor, pain, and sickness.
34. Baptism
35. The Blessed Virgin Mary
36. The Immaculate Conception
37. Sin we ourselves commit
38. Two, mortal and venial
39. A grievous offense against the law of God.
40. Because it takes away the life of the soul
41. Venial sin is a less serious offense against the law of God.
42. Our guardian angels will try to help us stay holy. They pray for us and our conscience tells us what we should not do.
43. Yes, God wants us to forgive others as He forgives us.
44. We can work to stay in a state of grace and pray for help from our guardian angels to help us avoid sin and go to heaven.

Part 2: Matching

1. C
2. D
3. E
4. B
5. A
6. J
7. H
8. I
9. F
10. G

Part 3: Completion

1. angels
2. happiness
3. prayers

4. soul
5. sanctifying grace
6. original
7. actual
8. Mortal sin
9. The Blessed Virgin Mary
10. Venial
11. things
12. second
13. spirit.
14. sees
15. Father
16. Divine.
17. God
18. Redeemer
19. mystery
20. secret

Part 4: Yes or No

1. Yes
2. Yes
3. Yes
4. No
5. Yes
6. Yes
7. Yes
8. Yes
9. Yes
10. No
11. Yes
12. Yes
13. No
14. Yes
15. No

Chapter 3

Lesson 31

Questions
1, 3, 4, 5, 6, 7, 8

To Prove My Mastery, Lessons 20–31

Part 1. Short Answer

1. Adam and Eve
2. Abraham and Moses
3. Yes, they had to wait for thousands of years
4. The Jews prepared by praying, obeying God, and offering sacrifices.
5. Offering God a gift or a victim, such as a lamb.
6. The victim was placed on an altar, if an animal it was killed and its blood sprinkled on the altar. The victim was then burned.
7. To adore God, to thank God, to make up for sin, and to ask God for His favors.
8. The Angel Gabriel came to Mary at the Annunciation and asked her.
9. Mary's cousin.
10. In a stable in Bethlehem
11. Over two thousand years ago
12. Some shepherds
13. Gold, frankincense, and myrrh.
14. Forty days old
15. In Jerusalem
16. Simeon
17. To flee from Herod who had ordered the death of all babies under the age of two.
18. King Herod
19. An angel
20. Nazareth
21. Answers will vary

Part 2: Yes or No

1. Yes
2. No
3. Yes
4. No
5. Yes

Part 3: Completion

1. angel
2. altar
3. Gabriel
4. Adam
5. Elizabeth

Part 4: Multiple Choice

1. B
2. B
3. A
4. C

Part 5: Matching

1. B
2. D
3. E
4. A
5. G
6. C
7. I
8. J
9. H
10. F

Chapter 4

Lesson 42

Questions

1. Answers will vary.
2. We can attend Mass.
3. To remember the sacrifice Jesus made for us.
4. Because He redeemed us through His sacrifice on the cross.
5. Because they knew they would be allowed into heaven soon.
6. Because Christ's suffering was caused by sin and it shows how much our sins hurt Jesus.

To Prove My Mastery, Lessons 32–42

Part 1. Short Answer

1. About thirty years old
2. John the Baptist
3. Because Jesus is also human and can be tempted, even if He is without sin.
4. The wedding feast at Cana
5. To affirm His identity as God the Son
6. Jerusalem
7. On the feast of Passover
8. The power to say Mass
9. On Holy Thursday at the Last Supper
10. On Holy Thursday at the Last Supper
11. On Mount Calvary outside Jerusalem
12. Good Friday
13. To redeem mankind by dying for our sins
14. First, He offered Himself to adore God for us. Second, He offered Himself to thank God for all His favors to us. Third, He offered Himself to God to make up for our sins. Fourth, He offered Himself to ask God's blessings and favors for all men.
15. Three days
16. In limbo
17. It is an unbloody sacrifice of Jesus' death and resurrection.

18. Offertory, Consecration, Communion
19. Because it is God offering himself for us.
20. Yes, they are the same sacrifice
21. On Easter Sunday
22. At the Ascension
23. On the last day, Judgment day.

Part 2: Completion

1. Easter Sunday
2. Palm Sunday
3. Holy Eucharist
4. Calvary
5. Good Friday
6. Ascension Day
7. Apostles
8. Last Supper

Part 3

1. B, D

Part 4: Answer Yes or No

1. Yes
2. Yes
3. No
4. Yes
5. No
6. Yes

Part 5: Multiple Choice

1. B
2. A
3. C
4. C

Chapter 5

Lesson 51

Questions

1. By offering all her actions to God
2. a. Sanctifying Grace
   b. Sanctifying Grace
   c. Actual Grace
   d. Actual Grace
   e. Sanctifying Grace
   e. Actual Grace
   f. Actual Grace
3. a, b, c

To Prove My Mastery, Lessons 43–51

Part 1. Short Answer

1. Grace is a supernatural gift from God
2. God, the Holy Spirit
3. The principal ways of obtaining grace are prayer and the sacraments, especially the Holy Eucharist.
4. Actual and sanctifying Grace
5. It is a supernatural gift which makes us holy and pleasing to God.
6. Makes us adopted children of God and opens our souls to heaven.
7. Mortal sin
8. No, we need sanctifying grace to get to heaven.
9. A supernatural help of God which enlightens our mind and strengthens our will to do good and avoid evil.
10. Prayer, good works, and the sacraments
11. We only have actual grace when we need it, so it disappears when we do not need it.
12. Jesus
13. Holy Eucharist and Penance and Reconciliation

14. Faith, Hope, and Charity

Part 2: Completion

1. Holy Spirit
2. Jesus Christ
3. Church
4. sanctifying grace
5. God
6. sanctifying grace
7. actual grace
8. heaven
9. mortal sin

Part 3: Yes or No

1. Yes
2. Yes
3. No
4. No
5. No
6. No
7. No
8. Yes
9. Yes

Chapter 6

To Prove My Mastery, Lessons 52–57

Part 1. Short Answer

1. Pentecost
2. Jesus founded the Church to bring all men to eternal salvation.

3. The current pope
4. Answers will vary.
5. All baptized persons united in the same true faith, the same sacrifice, and the same sacraments, under the Holy Father.
6. One, holy, catholic, apostolic
7. The union of the faithful on earth, the blessed in heaven, and the souls in purgatory, with Christ as their head.
8. At our individual deaths
9. On the last day, judgment day
10. When Mary was brought body and soul into heaven

Part 2: Multiple Choice

1. B
2. C
3. C
4. A
5. A

Part 3: Completion

1. sanctifying grace
2. pope
3. faith
4. sacraments
5. sacrifice
6. one
7. actual grace
8. Holy Spirit
9. Catholic
10. purgatory

Part 4: Yes or No

1. Yes
2. No
3. Yes
4. Yes
5. No

Chapter 7

Lesson 65

Questions

1. c, d, e
2. b, c, e, f
3. a, b, i

To Prove My Mastery, Lessons 58–65

Part 1. Short Answer

1. By obeying his commandments
2. 1. I am the Lord thy God; thou shalt not have strange gods before me.
   2. Thou shalt not take the name of the Lord thy God in vain.
   3. Remember thou keep holy the Lord's day.
   4. Honor thy father and thy mother.
   5. Thou shalt not kill.
   6. Thou shalt not commit adultery.
   7. Thou shalt not steal.
   8. Thou shalt not bear false witness against thy neighbor.
   9. Thou shalt not covet thy neighbor's wife.
   10. Thou shalt not covet thy neighbor's goods.
3. God gave them to Moses who shared them.
4. Thou shalt love the Lord God with all thy heart, and thou shalt love thy neighbor as thyself.

5. By obeying the commandments about neighbors and by showing them love.
6. Worship only God
7. By acts of faith, hope and charity and by adoring and praising Him.
8. The Holy men and women who have joined God in heaven.
9. By asking them to pray on our behalf.
10. Raising our minds and hearts to God.
11. We must pray with our minds, hearts, and our words. We must mean what we say.
12. No, we must pray and know God if we want to know Him in heaven.
13. It tells us to speak in reverence of God and holy things.
14. Because it is a powerful name and by speaking reverently we show God respect.
15. By swearing, curing, making fun of God or holy things.
16. Keep Sunday holy.
17. Go to Church on Sundays and avoid unnecessary work.

Part 2: Yes or No

1. Yes
2. No
3. Yes
4. Yes
5. No

Part 3: Matching

1. D
2. A
3. B
4. C

Part 4: Multiple Choice

1. B
2. C
3. A
4. B
5. B

Part 5: Completion

1. Worship only God
2. using the Lord's name in vain
3. attend Mass

Image Credits

cover The Sacred Heart of Jesus, end of nineteenth century (mixed media), © Archives Charmet / Bridgeman Images

p2-3, 28-29, 68-69, 98-99, 132-133, 154-155, 178-179 Christ and Saint John the Baptist in Hagia Sophia (mosaic), Tarker / Bridgeman Images

px-1 The Creation of Adam, from The Story of Adam and Eve (oil on copper), Brueghel, Jan the Younger (1601-78), Photo © Christie's Images / Bridgeman Images

p3 God creating the sun, the moon and the stars in the Firmament, c.1650 (oil on copper), Brueghel, Jan the Younger (1601-78), Photo © Christie's Images / Bridgeman Images

p6 Jesus Teaching (gouache on paper), © Look and Learn / Bridgeman Images

p12 A girl confesses a sin to God, photo by ravipat/Shutterstock

p17 Golden monstrance, photo by MARI TERE/Shutterstock

p19 The Last Supper, Uptton, Clive (1911-2006), © Look and Learn / Bridgeman Images

p21 First Communion (aquatint), Leloir, Maurice (1853-1940), Look and Learn / Valerie Jackson Harris Collection / Bridgeman Images

p30 A free flying white dove, illustration by Elzza/Shutterstock

p33 Detail of the painting of the interior of the dome depicting the Holy Trinity, 1663-65 (fresco), Mignard, Pierre (1612-95), © Clement Guillaume / Bridgeman Images

p36 Creation (colour litho), © Look and Learn / Bridgeman Images

p38 Archangel Michael Sculpture, photo by aSuruwataRi/Shutterstock

p41 A vintage angel illustration, c1890, image by Victorian Traditions/ Shutterstock

p44 Eve giving Adam the forbidden fruit (photo), Godong / Bridgeman Images

p46 Red apple with bite taken, photo by Weerachai Khamfu/ Shutterstock

p47 Marble statue of the Virgin of Sorrow, photo by Kamira/Shutterstock

p51 The death of Abel (coloured engraving), © Look and Learn / Bridgeman Images

p58 Boys playing soccer, photo by Robert Kneschke/Shutterstock

p66-67 Adoration of the Shepherds, 1689 (oil on canvas), Le Brun, Charles (1619-90), Bridgeman Images
p68 Statue of Jesus Christ with Sacred Heart, photo by Meryll/ Shutterstock
p71 Abraham (engraving), © Look and Learn / Bridgeman Images
p73 King David by Adamo Tadolini on the base of the Colonna dell'Immacolata, Rome Italy, photo by Only Fabrizio/Shutterstock
p76 The Annunciation, 1644 (oil on canvas), Champaigne, Philippe de (1602-74), © Ferens Art Gallery / Bridgeman Images
p78 The Visitation, 1491 (tempera on panel), Ghirlandaio, Domenico (Domenico Bigordi) (1449-94), Bridgeman Images
p80-81 La Nativite De Notre Seigneur, Peinture murale d'apres Hipp Flandrin, St Germain des Pres, a Paris (chromolitho), © Look and Learn / Bridgeman Images
p82 The Christmas Story: The Shepherds' Tale (gouache on paper), Watt, John Millar (1895-1975), © Look and Learn / Bridgeman Images
p84 Simeon and the infant Jesus (colour litho), © Look and Learn / Bridgeman Images
p86 Three Wise Men (gouache on paper), Watt, John Millar (1895-1975), © Look and Learn / Bridgeman Images
p90 Jesus is found in the Temple (coloured engraving), © Look and Learn / Bridgeman Images
p99 The Baptism of Christ (gouache on paper), © Look and Learn / Bridgeman Images
p101 The Temptation of Christ (1854), Ary Scheffer (1795–1858), public domain via Wikimedia Commons
p105 The Marriage Feast at Cana, detail of Christ and musicians, c.1562 (oil on canvas), Veronese, (Paolo Caliari) (1528-88), Bridgeman Images
p107 The Miracle of the Five Loaves (coloured engraving), © Look and Learn / Bridgeman Images
p109 Palm leaf, photo by COLOA Studio/Shutterstock
p111 The Last Supper (oil on panel), Macip, Vicente Juan (Juan de Juanes) (c.1510-79), Bridgeman Images
p112 Priest celebrates Mass, photo by wideonet/Shutterstock
p115 Christ on the cross, the Three Marys on mourning by John and the Donor or Patron, 1514, by Pier Francesco Sacchi, called Il Pavese (1485-1528), Tarker / Bridgeman Images

p118 The Last Supper (oil on panel), Macip, Vicente Juan (Juan de Juanes) (c.1510-79), Bridgeman Images
p120 The Resurrection, 15th century (tempera on panel), Master of the Osservanza, (fl.c.1436), Founders Society Purchase / Gift of Mr & Mrs Henry Ford II / Bridgeman Images
p123 The Ascension of Christ (colour litho), © Look and Learn / Bridgeman Images
p130-131 The Descent of the Holy Spirit, Mura, Francesco de (1696-1782), Photo © Bonhams, London, UK / Bridgeman Images
p133 Holy Spirit symbol, illustration by Thoom/Shutterstock
p143 Mary receiving the gifts of the Holy Spirit, detail (tempera on wood), Master of Lluca (13th century), © Iberfoto / Bridgeman Images
p147 Catholic girl praying, photo by Africa Studio/Shutterstock
p149 The Good Samaritan (gouache on paper), © Look and Learn / Bridgeman Images
p155 The window of a cathedral of St. Peter in Vatican, with a dove representing the holy spirit, photo by Dan Costa/Shutterstock
p158 Giving of the Keys to St. Peter, from the Sistine Chapel, 1481 (fresco), Perugino, Pietro (c.1445-1523), Bridgeman Images
p164-165 The Forerunners of Christ with Saints and Martyrs, 1423-24 (egg tempera on wood), Angelico, Fra (Guido di Pietro/Giovanni da Fiesole) (c.1387-1455), Bridgeman Images
p167 Autumn maple leaves falling down, photo by Valentina Razumova/ Shutterstock
p170 The Assumption of Mary (chromolitho), © Look and Learn / Bridgeman Images
p177 The Assumption of the Virgin Mary, 1642, by Guido Reni (1575-1642), Tarker / Bridgeman Images
p179 The sermon on the mount, Copping, Harold (1863-1932), © Look and Learn / Bridgeman Images
p180 Stone tablets, illustration by Robert J. Beyers II/Shutterstock
p182 Moses and the Ten Commandments, Uptton, Clive (1911-2006), © Look and Learn / Bridgeman Images
p188 Golden crucifix, photo by gdvcom/Shutterstock
p196 Family arriving to Mass, photo by Rawpixel/Shutterstock
p203 Moses receiving the Ten Commandments from God on Mount Sinai (colour litho), © Look and Learn / Bridgeman Images

p208 The Virgin in Prayer, 1640-50 (oil on canvas), Sassoferrato, Il (Giovanni Battista Salvi) (1609-85), Bridgeman Images
p213 St Michael (chromolitho), © Look and Learn / Bridgeman Images
p215 The Immaculate Conception with the Fifteen Mysteries of the Rosary (oil on canvas), Cabrera, Miguel (1695-1768), Photo © Christie's Images / Bridgeman Images
p216 Interior of a Scriptorium, School of Segovia (oil on panel), Bridgeman Images